WHERE POWER STOPS

DAVID RUNCIMAN is professor of politics at Cambridge University and the former head of the department of politics and international studies. He is the author of six previous books, including *How Democracy Ends* (Profile), *Political Hypocrisy*, *The Confidence Trap* and *Politics* (for the *Ideas in Profile* series). He writes regularly about politics for the *London Review of Books* and hosts the widely acclaimed weekly podcast *Talking Politics*.

WHERE POWER STOPS

The Making and Unmaking of Presidents and Prime Ministers

DAVID RUNCIMAN

P

PROFILE BOOKS

This paperback edition revised and updated in 2020

First published in Great Britain in 2019 by
Profile Books Ltd
29 Cloth Fair
London ECIA 7JQ

www.profilebooks.com

1 3 5 7 9 10 8 6 4 2

Typeset in Dante by MacGuru Ltd
Printed and bound in Great Britain by
CPI Group (UK) Ltd, Croydon CRO 4YY

A CIP catalogue record for this book is available from the British Library.

ISBN 978 1 78816 334 7
eISBN 978 1 78283 599 8

CONTENTS

INTRODUCTION

WHERE POWER STOPS

THERE IS A STORY that often gets told about modern presidents and prime ministers, and sometimes gets told by them as well. The politician spends half a lifetime working tirelessly towards the top job, with the goal of making a real difference once he or she gets there. These politicians are driven by personal ambition, of course, but they also harbour genuine hopes of doing some good. Then, when they finally reach the summit, they discover that the power of the office is nowhere near what they had assumed. They issue their instructions. Dutiful officials nod along encouragingly. But nothing really changes. Once the door to the Oval Office or No. 10 closes behind them, and they settle their feet under the desk, the new president or prime minister finds out that it's just another room and just another desk. It feels like true power is still somewhere out of reach.

An emblematic version of this tale is recounted by Jonathan Powell in his book *The New Machiavelli*. Powell was Tony Blair's chief of staff in Downing Street, and he saw at first hand his boss's frustrations with the limits of his ability to get things done. Powell describes Blair's enthusiasm, on becoming prime minister, for undertaking an immediate programme of reform. He wanted to start making a difference straight away. But the more he agitated for change, the less responsive the machinery of government proved to be. There was an empty space where Blair had believed his prime ministerial authority would reside. 'The new Prime Minister pulls on the levers of power,' Powell writes, 'and nothing happens.' It wasn't just Blair, and it's not just prime ministers. George W. Bush prided himself on his ability to make a decision. But according to those who worked closely with him, Bush never learned that just because he was president it didn't follow that his decisions would turn into actions. Too often he was deciding into the void.

Usually, these stories are presented as a kind of morality tale. In politics you should never assume that there is a pot of gold at the end of the rainbow. It's better to know how little is waiting for you, like a weird inversion of the parable of the Wizard of Oz. In place of the Yellow Brick Road is the greasy pole, which has to be ascended to reach the Emerald City. Yet the successful climber finds that his or her fate is not to encounter a shrunken wizard at the end of it. Instead it is to become that person: the impostor behind the curtain.

||||

How do politicians react when they discover themselves in that position? Some, like Bush, never quite acknowledge it. Others, like Blair, decide to do something about it. Blair concluded that he had to build the machinery that would enable his administration to deliver on its ambitions. He called this instrument 'the Delivery Unit'. It was designed to make sure that the levers in Downing Street were connected to the rest of government. Yet, even after ten years in power, Blair was frustrated with how little he had managed to achieve. One reason he was reluctant to leave office at the end was a nagging feeling that he was only just beginning to get the hang of it. Real power still felt out of reach, somewhere over the horizon. Since quitting front-line politics, Blair has made himself into a salesman for the idea of 'Deliverology', which promises to help politicians around the world with the problem of actually getting things done. It's a pretty threadbare prospectus. Perma-tanned and increasingly wizened, Blair cuts a tawdry figure these days. Here is another version of the morality tale. The wizard has spent so long behind the curtain that he doesn't realise how diminished he appears when he steps out in front.

There are other ways of responding to the deficit of power at the summit of politics. The truly paranoid politician believes that the reason the levers are not working is that someone has cut the strings. Faced with the frustrations of office, it is always tempting to imagine that there is a conspiracy at work to prevent meaningful change. Blame it on the 'deep state' – or, in the politer British version, on 'Sir Humphrey'. Probably no one is immune from this suspicion, especially in the long reaches of the night. All the politicians I write about in this book had moments when they believed that dark forces were at work to prevent them getting their way. But only one has turned this belief into his governing philosophy. Donald Trump's response to any setback is to claim that he is the victim of a deliberate attempt to subvert his authority. He cannot accept that there are inherent limits to the power of his office. So any manifestations of those limits become further evidence of the conspiracy against him. These are the dangers of electing a confirmed narcissist to an office that is not as powerful as it seems.

That said, it is not true that none of the levers works. Some do, all too well. Another temptation is to keep pulling until you find one that produces a direct response. Inevitably, for both presidents and prime ministers, this tends to be the lever that links to the armed forces. Again, Blair is emblematic here, but he is far from unusual. Chastened by his inability to get traction with his domestic agenda, Blair latched gratefully on to the opportunity presented by 9/11 to turn himself into a player on the international stage. It wasn't just that he wanted to put the world to rights according to his own lights. It was also that he was able to do so, more easily than he could put his own government right, because the instrument to hand was military force. The same was true of Bush. But it has equally been true of politicians as otherwise different from each other as Thatcher and Clinton, Obama and Trump. The power of the office they hold is least constrained when it comes to taking action abroad. As I write now, Trump, who promised to extricate the US from the Middle East, has just ordered the assassination by drone of Iran's top general. Why did he do it? In part, just because he could. This is why presidents and prime ministers, who almost never get elected on a foreign policy platform, often find that foreign policy is what ends up defining their tenure at the top. The international arena is where they can make the biggest difference, for better or for worse.

The trauma of 9/11 – and what followed – reveals another fundamental truth. The power of presidents and prime ministers is hugely dependent on the accidents of history. For Thatcher, the Falklands War completely altered what it was possible for her to achieve in office. Without the Argentine invasion of April 1982, over which she had no control, her premiership would have been very different. For Gordon Brown, the financial crisis of 2007–8 reconfigured what he could accomplish, as it did for Obama's presidency. Such unforeseen events do not suddenly endow presidents and prime ministers with superpowers: the frustrations of trying to get things done remain just as intense (as both Brown and Obama discovered). But they do provide an opportunity to break out of a rut.

Obama's one-time chief of staff Rahm Emanuel is credited with coining the memorable line 'Never let a crisis go to waste'. Elected leaders chafing against the limits of their power can take comfort from the thought that something is bound to turn up that will alter their situation. That is often why they cling on, even past the point when it would appear easier to give up. It is why, for instance, Theresa May clung on after the 2017 British general election and through the countless months of Brexit travails that followed. As they say of the weather in

Texas – if you don't like it, just stick around. But as with the weather in Texas, it isn't all that reassuring to know change is coming. It doesn't leave you any more in control of your fate.

There is one further response available to politicians who find that high office feels like getting access to a control panel that no one has bothered to plug in. They can reject the premise that lies behind the metaphor. The mistake is to think of the exercise of power as like operating a machine. It isn't levers you push and pull to get things done: it's people. The instruments of politics are human beings, and it is their hopes and fears, their resilience and their frailty, that you have to operate on. A successful president or prime minister needs to know, above all else, what it is that makes other people tick. That's why this book starts with the presidency of Lyndon Baines Johnson, the master manipulator of human weakness.

||||
||||

LBJ is a hero to many contemporary politicians, from across the political spectrum. Why? Because he showed that it is possible to escape the fable of the Wizard of Oz. Johnson went behind the curtain and, notwithstanding the empty space he found there, decided that he would make things happen anyway. First as Majority Leader in the US Senate, then as President, Johnson achieved his goals by his ruthlessness, his relentlessness, his attention to detail and the sheer force of his political personality. Johnson passed the legislation that had defeated his predecessors, including the great civil rights reforms of the mid-1960s. He did it despite not believing in it (or at least, as a lifelong Southern racist, never having shown any sign of believing it). He did it in part simply to prove that he could. He threatened and bribed, he caressed and cajoled, he literally pushed and pulled his fellow politicians – Johnson rarely met anyone without giving them a hug or a tug with his big, bearlike hands – until they bent to his will. Johnson is the politician other politicians look to when they want reassurance that anything is possible if you set your mind to it. And so long as you don't have too many scruples.

As heroes go, Johnson remains profoundly flawed. He was an exceptional politician, but he did not buck the wider trends that bedevil lesser leaders. He was extraordinarily dependent on his good fortune: the presidency came his way not by his own efforts but because of the terrible fate that struck down his predecessor, John F. Kennedy, who may have been on the brink of dispensing with Johnson's services before his assassination. Johnson was a vicious and paranoid man, prone to lashing out at enemies real and imagined. He invariably suspected that the political establishment was plotting against him; often he was right. His signal achievements were in domestic policy, but he too was unable to resist the temptations that came his way to wade in overseas. Johnson's tragedy was that he did not need a war to make the office of president live up to its billing. He had already done that by his own efforts. But he dared not retreat from the war in Vietnam he inherited for fear of appearing weak. So he kept pulling at that lever long after he knew he should stop.

The other reason why Johnson looms so large – over this book and over the recent history of political leadership – is because of an additional piece of good fortune. Johnson has been lucky in his biographer. The heroic figure worshipped by so many aspiring politicians is the one who emerges from Robert Caro's epic four-volume life of Johnson (the fifth and final volume is still to come), which has become required reading for would-be leaders. Caro's LBJ is the ultimate up-by-his-boot-straps politico, a man who masters his destiny by mastering all those who come within his orbit. Caro shows how Johnson conquered each political institution he reached by learning its rules and then learning how to make them work to his advantage, starting with local politics in Texas, then on to Washington, up through the House and the Senate, and ultimately arriving at the presidency itself. LBJ made the political weather wherever he went, and many people now read Caro to try to find out how.

Caro's thesis is that, as Johnson rose in politics, we discover more and more of who he really was. So when he finally reached the most powerful position of all, we get to see the person behind the political mask. As president, Johnson's racism fell away and his essential compassion for the oppressed and the dispossessed came through. Power corrupts, as Caro acknowledges, but 'what is seldom said, but what is equally true, is that power also *reveals*'. The highest office reveals the true nature of the man. It's a nice idea. But I don't buy it. Instead, I think almost the opposite is the case. The presidency didn't show us some essential truth about Johnson. But Johnson shows us some essential truths about the presidency.

Like most politicians, Johnson's character was pretty set by the time he reached the top. He didn't change as president. He was the same unscrupulous, driven, opportunistic, cruel, avaricious, sentimental, domineering, capacious, compelling, faintly monstrous figure he had always been, even as a young man. What was different were the circumstances in which he found himself. At each stage of his career that distinctive personality probed and tested the limits of power, looking for outlets for his desire to dominate. Where he found them reveals what can be done by a president – and also what can't. Johnson's personality works like the political equivalent of a barium dye, passing through the corridors of power and illuminating the hidden passages and concealed blockages that would otherwise be almost impossible for an outsider to detect. America's political institutions have never been laid so bare as they are by Caro, even though he is ostensibly just writing the life of a man. That is what political biography can do: once we understand the character of the person, we can follow that character behind the curtain and get to see what is really there.

In this book I write about Johnson and eight other recent American presidents and British prime ministers (along with one would-be president who never made it, John Edwards, for reasons I'll explain shortly). In each case I start from the premise that the personality of the politician helps explain the scope and the limitations of the office. None of these people was fundamentally changed by their time in power. The person who arrives at the summit of politics is recognisably the same as the person who comes down from it. Who they really are was set well in advance. What changes are the circumstances in which they find themselves and their expectation of what can be done while they are there.

The presidents and prime ministers I describe here are readily identifiable as the people they were when much younger. Their childhoods did much to shape their political futures, and so did their educations. Thatcher, Blair and May all went to Oxford, and the subsequent careers of each cannot be understood without seeing how differently they experienced student life. Each of their premierships was an extension of what they learned at university, not just about how the world works but also about how they might fit into it. It is also striking how many of these politicians saw themselves as future leaders from a very young age. All of them were capable of envisaging themselves in high office, no matter how remote from it they were. The teenage Theresa May, growing up in a Gloucestershire vicarage, truly believed she would be prime minister one day. This was a ridiculous idea. It was also entirely correct.

There is a selection bias here. I do not – with the exception of Edwards – write about any of those many thousands of individuals who also believed they would lead their countries one day but never made it, or even came close. But the fact that the subjects of these essays were the exceptionally lucky ones does nothing to diminish the importance of their sense of destiny. If you have a dream and it comes true, remembering that other people's dreams usually don't will not make your experiences feel less remarkable. If anything, it makes them even more so.

The source material for these stories varies from case to case. Some come from memoirs written by the leaders themselves (Blair, Brown, Cameron). Some are from books written by colleagues or friends (Clinton speaking with Taylor Branch, Obama as described by Ben Rhodes). Some are the work of sympathetic biographers (Caro on Johnson, Charles Moore on Thatcher). Some are from semi-hostile biographies (Rosa Prince on May) or even from what are little more than hatchet jobs (Bob Woodward on Trump, Tom Bower on Blair). Yet it is striking how consistently the theme of character being destiny comes through in each of them. It is not just Johnson's personality that works as a kind of barium dye. Once we get to see the type of person we are dealing with, we start to get a picture of the true shape of their political power. Inevitably, the dye reveals a different trace in each case. Where the power stops shifts as different political personalities come and go. In that sense, reading Caro as a how-to guide for political leadership is probably a mistake. Only LBJ can do what LBJ did. But in seeing how it was done, we get to understand the limits of the possible.

There are a few other broader lessons we can draw. It helps to arrive in office knowing who you are. Johnson's preternatural calm on the day of Kennedy's assassination – when his long foretold destiny suddenly came into focus – is the ultimate example of how self-knowledge may be the most valuable political commodity of all. This is not the same as having a sense of self-worth. Johnson probably never got over a feeling of inadequacy, despite all his extraordinary accomplishments. It was what drove him. Obama, always poised and self-contained, knew his own worth full well. Yet he accomplished less as a result, because he never really pushed the limits of what he could achieve. Thatcher, despite her reputation for knowing her own mind, was surprisingly fragile in her confidence and scatty in her convictions. Yet she understood, with an almost uncanny instinct, what someone with her personality could achieve as prime minister, especially when the occasion arose. She did not know much about the country she governed. But she knew how to seize her moment when the chance came to govern it.

Blair was far more self-confident and sure of what he believed than Thatcher was. But it did him little good. He persisted in trying to make the office of prime minister suit his convictions rather than trying to adapt those convictions to the limits of what the office made possible. Clinton was perhaps the most intelligent man ever to occupy the Oval Office. His mind was voracious, almost carnal in its appetite for new information and fresh insights. It was too much. He couldn't contain the intelligence he had within the space of the role he occupied. It spilled out, and too often it went nowhere.

It is sometimes said that it doesn't do for a president or prime minister to be too smart: a second-class mind is more likely to make for a first-class leader. Like many such generalisations about politics, there's some truth to it, but also plenty that it misses. There are lots of different ways for a politician to be intelligent, and there are many things that politicians can know which are unknown to anyone on the outside. What matters is whether they know what it is that they know. And if they do, whether they understand what that knowledge is good for.

||||

This brings us to Trump. If Johnson is where this book starts, Trump represents a troubling place to end up, and not just because his story is not yet done. Does he fit the broader patterns of political leadership I describe here, or is he somehow outside them? In many ways, Trump exemplifies the idea that the personality of the politician reveals the character of the office he occupies. Trump's persona is not going to change. He is unnervingly consistent to what he has always been: showman, chauvinist, charlatan. What he is doing is testing how far a man like that is able to push the boundaries of what a president can be. He has been more successful than many people believed was possible. His willingness to say anything – and possibly to believe anything – in order to get his way turns out to be a surprisingly effective means of maximising his authority. Given that a majority of Americans revile him, he has done quite a lot with the limited power he has. Perhaps he too bucks the fable of the Wizard of Oz. He simply refuses to acknowledge the existence of the curtain. He wants people to see!

What makes Trump so unnerving, however, is his seeming lack of any self-knowledge. He is not really probing for the limits of what the presidency allows, because that would require him to accept that there are limits. He does what he does regardless. The Trump I write about here is both more and less than a president should be. More, because he is behaving as though his power were truly as he believes it to be. Less, because he is also behaving as though the presidency were just another job (businessman, reality TV host, mafia boss). Much of the time he does not seem to appreciate where he is. None of the other politicians I write about is anything like as cavalier as Trump, or anything like as erratic. Why would someone whose personality is so fixed be so unpredictable in office? Because that personality makes him incapable of seeing the presidency as its previous occupants have seen it, as an office that comes with certain expectations of how to behave. Trump is, in institutional terms, unhinged.

Does that mean he is mentally unfit to be president? During his time in the White House Trump has been dogged by repeated rumours about his intellectual incapacity – he has been variously described as a 'fucking moron', 'like an eleven-year-old child', a 'dope', an 'idiot' and 'dumb as shit'. And that's just how his former aides and colleagues speak about him. Plenty of psychiatrists have pushed back hard against the so-called 'Goldwater rule', which prevents them from diagnosing the psychological failings of public figures at second hand. For many, this injunction bars them from simply stating the obvious: Trump is out of his mind.

But we should be wary of assuming that this is enough to place Trump beyond the pale of conventional political leadership. Most of those I write about here have had their sanity questioned. Blair was widely thought to have lost his mental bearings during and after the Iraq War. Brown was pursued by stories of titanic rages and prolonged depressions. I have spoken to people who believe that the true story of May's premiership has been suppressed, given that as a type-1 diabetic she faces potentially serious cognitive handicaps, including an inability either to process new information or to change her mind. That would explain her futile version of Brexit! These kinds of accusation come with the territory: presidents and prime ministers are often thought to be psychologically undone by office. It is one of the ways we express our discomfort with anyone aspiring to that kind of power.

Max Weber, writing one hundred years ago, made the case that the risk of madness is not simply an accidental by-product of high office. It is an essential part of it: a feature, not a bug. Presidents and prime ministers have to deal with the mental strain of bearing enormous political responsibility without necessarily having the personal authority to match. The leaders of modern states hold the lives of millions in their hands, and yet they often can't even get the people in the next room to do what they want. It might make anyone a little crazy. Leadership is a constant tug of war between the rules of political accountability and the law of unintended consequences. That has not changed in the time since Weber wrote. One reason it is so hard to be a president or a prime minister is that the voters hold the wizard responsible for what happens. Even though the wizard is just the impostor behind the curtain.

By far the sanest president or prime minister of recent times was Obama. He went out of his way to maintain an even keel, even in the face of the most outrageous provocation. He made sure that he stayed connected with his family and that he got enough downtime. Is it possible to be too sane for the presidency? Certainly there were moments when Obama's insistence on keeping his cool looked like a missed opportunity. Sometimes one longed to see him let rip. But that was not his style. Nor was it what got him elected.

This is the other deep tension that resides in the character of anyone who pursues the highest office. The personality traits that can win you the crucial election may not be the ones that suit the role to which you have been elected. Campaigning, as the slogan goes, is not governing. Obama the candidate was known to his inner circle as '"No drama" Obama'. During his long, bruising, underdog campaign in 2008 to wrest the Democratic nomination from Hillary Clinton, and then for the duration of the shorter but equally high-wire act needed to win a general election that was taking place as the world economy was having a heart attack, his level temperament was a golden asset. Refusing to get ruffled got him over the line. But when he became president he needed other skills too. His preference for cool analysis over impulsive decision-making and his insistence that he would not be baited by his baying opponents – as his wife, Michelle, memorably said in 2016, 'when they go low, we go high' – were still assets. But they were not enough.

Personal development is very difficult over the course of a political career, especially when being who you are has made you what you have become. Why would political leaders whose approach to politics won them office abandon that approach once they get there? Trump stormed to the Republican nomination and ultimately the presidency in 2016 with a scorched earth campaign that recognised no limits and took no prisoners. He defeated his rivals by mocking them, belittling them and, when the opportunity arose, lying about them. That is how he has carried on conducting himself as president, to continuing howls of outrage from his opponents. But who is to say he is wrong? If high office doesn't change who politicians really are, we shouldn't expect it to change how it makes it behave.

Some politicians reach the top without having to win an election to get there. It was Johnson's misfortune, until it became his good fortune, that his temperament made him a terrible presidential candidate, with a record of abject failure before he finally inherited the top job by chance. He failed as a national candidate because he could not adjust the manipulative and Machiavellian skill set that had served him so well in the Senate to the people-pleasing demands of a presidential campaign. But becoming president by default meant that he did not have to adjust who he was in order to reach the Oval Office, where that skill set served him well again. Once it was time for him to fight an election in his own right in 1964, he had already shown he could get things done. The job of president suited him, despite his being fundamentally unsuited to winning it.

Theresa May also reached the top without fighting a general election in her own right. When she faced one in 2017, by choice rather than by necessity, the skill set that had got her to Downing Street let her down. The tenacious, colourless, undeviating politician who tiptoed over the corpses to inherit the crown in the aftermath of Brexit morphed on the campaign trail into the deathless Maybot: cold, mechanical and seemingly without a personality of her own. Jeremy Corbyn, a politician for whom campaigning had been the lifeblood of his entire career, ran rings round her. Nevertheless, May somehow survived the experience, and her premiership was kept afloat for two more years by the dutiful doggedness that remained her calling card as a politician.

Change is hard for politicians. But what makes political leadership so precarious is that it is relatively easy for voters.

If we get tired of our politicians, we can get rid of them. The qualities that we once appreciated in a leader can turn surprisingly quickly into what we loathe about them. LBJ's deviousness caught up with him in the end. Blair's sincerity came to seem like sanctimony. Obama's coolness turned into aloofness. May's steadfastness made her come across like a robot. Corbyn's simplicity of purpose, which served him so well in 2017, betrayed him in the general election of 2019, when it came to seem like obstinacy and perhaps even idiocy. Another truism of democratic life is that all political careers end in failure. Perhaps it would be easier to say that no political personality is built to last at the very top. The demands of the highest office are never fixed.

Yet if there is one quality that is indispensable for anyone at or near the summit of political life, it is stamina. This does not have to be physical stamina, though that helps. Corbyn had a reputation for being a lazy politician, taking time off in lieu whenever he was expected to record a TV interview on a Sunday. He rarely strayed outside his comfort zone. But there was nothing lazy about his political career. As a backbench MP he stuck it out for decades, even when he had very little to show for it. Corbyn hung in there, where others might have given up. As a result, he was still around when his chance came. In the end, he could not take the ultimate chance he was offered to become Prime Minister. But the fact he even came close in 2017 is testament to his tenacity, which is a necessary condition of political success, even if it is not a sufficient one. Nevertheless, what Corbyn and May have in common, and in spades, is resilience. Another way of describing an inflexible political personality is to call it durability.

The British and US political systems are different, so the kinds of chances they throw up for resilient politicians will be different too. The presidency is open to genuine outsiders in a way that the prime ministership is not. No one could reach No. 10, as Trump reached the White House, without ever having stood for election before in any capacity. A presidential campaign, running over two or more years, with its relentless requirements for fundraising and attention-seeking, makes distinctive demands. It suits personalities as different as Obama's and Trump's – the one unflappable, the other unembarrassable. It would not suit someone like May. British politics is more self-contained, its campaigns shorter and the role of its parliament in selecting political leaders much more pronounced. Corbyn, in turning Labour into a mass movement that downplays the role of its elected MPs, is as close to an outsider as British politics has ever had near its summit. Yet he has had no career outside Parliament.

This book includes one story of political failure that could only happen in the US: the spectacular rise and fall of John Edwards. I tell it here because it illustrates some of the downsides of political resilience. Edwards was able to keep his eyes on the prize even as his personal life was falling apart. His ability to disconnect his public persona from his private experiences was an extreme version of what all political leaders have to go through. Yet it was so extreme that it highlights how absurd the exercise can become. There is a point past which the determination to keep going becomes its own form of madness. Edwards reached it, and then some.

The 2008 election cycle, in which Edwards had a second stab at reaching the White House after having been John Kerry's running mate four years earlier, provides a case study in the terrible toll the game of democratic thrones can take on its players. Obama's extraordinary mental stability in that campaign stands in stark contrast to the carnage that unfolded all around him. The Republican presidential nominee John McCain chose as his vice-presidential candidate Sarah Palin, the untested and relatively unknown Governor of Alaska.

Palin had a number of political qualities, including great gifts as a sassy stump orator ('That hopey, changey thing, how's it working out for y'all?'). But she was completely out of her depth as a candidate for national office. When her basic ignorance of the world became clear to everyone, including herself, she had a kind of mental breakdown. Yet she somehow made it through to the election and out the other side. She was still around to help booster Trump on his way to the White House in 2016. She may have fallen apart, but she did not change.

The people who have to change are the ones who get caught up in the chaos and end up as collateral damage. Palin's family paid the biggest price for her over-exposure. So did the family of John Edwards, along with his inner circle. It was Edwards's long-time fixer and one-time friend Andrew Young who ended up having to turn his life upside down to keep his boss's political show on the road. The indignities visited on Young – which culminated in his going on the run with Edwards's mistress, having been falsely identified by the candidate as the father of her child, who was in fact his own – are incredible but they are not inexplicable. His story reminds us that what lies behind any prominent political career are other people's lives, often in tatters. Leaders operate on human beings. They can chew them up and spit them out as well.

Trump is once again both the exception and the rule. His stamina remains an underrated weapon in his political arsenal. He didn't just outfight his opponents in 2016, he outlasted them, withstanding setbacks that would have felled a less resilient candidate. His appetite for gruelling speaking engagements in front of vast crowds has not diminished since he won the presidency. In fact, he seems happiest when he is hammering away at the podium. He has chewed up and spat out a remarkable number of staffers and one-time political allies in his relatively short political career, leaving many of their careers in ruins. He seems to measure his political success in large part by the number of bodies he can pile up at his door, regardless of their

prior allegiances. By that measure, he may be the most successful president in modern American history.

What makes him different, though, is his willingness to
turn his personal frustrations into the primary vehicle of his
political programme. He is the Complainer-in-Chief. Winning
the presidency did nothing to temper his feelings of grievance.
If anything, it amplified them. All presidents and prime ministers have periods when they feel that they are victims, despite
being the most powerful person in the land. Johnson, Thatcher,
Blair, Clinton, Brown, Obama, Cameron and May certainly
have had times of feeling sorry for themselves like that. But
none of them – not even for a moment – made victimhood
their raison d'être. They knew that such a move would be fatal
to their political authority – the whining, preening egomaniac
is not someone who can command the respect of the voters.
And without respect the president or prime minister is surely
lost. Yet Trump has shown, for now, that they were wrong.

iiii

The chapters of this book are stories about individuals, and no
two individuals are the same. I am not trying to supply my own
overarching morality tale. I hope that the moral of each story
speaks for itself. But Trump raises one fundamental question
that cuts across the whole period of politics covered by this
book, from the 1960s to the 2010s. That question is a simple
one: is it over?

Ours is now an age of populism. Democratic politics
around the world is being roiled by public anger. Much of this
anger is a manifestation of the deep anxieties and frustrations
that come from living through a period of relative economic
stagnation coupled with dramatic technological change. That
has been the story of the last ten years, at least. The rage gets
directed against politics and politicians because many voters
have become hyper-attuned to what they see as the inertia of

their political institutions and the tendency of their political class towards complacency at best and corruption at worst. In Britain and the US this has produced two signal outcomes: Brexit and Trump.

Something that connects British and US politics is that their systems are based on the principle of first-past-the-post – or winner-takes-all. It generates binary options. When offered a straight choice between the ways things have been and the chance to do something different, voters in both countries – albeit by narrow margins – have recently plumped for change-with-the-risk-of-chaos over continuity-with-the-risk-of-nothing-changing. It seems unlikely that people in the UK and the US are notably angrier than they are elsewhere. But the electoral idiosyncrasies of the two democracies have made these outcomes the emblems of the populist age.

As a result, it is now the voters who are testing the limits of the power of presidents and prime ministers as much as it is the politicians themselves. Brexit and Trump have acted as a litmus test that reveals things that were previously hidden about the countries that produced them. We turn out to be divided in new ways – between old and young, educated and less educated, connected and disconnected, 'somewheres' and 'anywheres' – and often to be as angry with each other as we are with the people who govern us. The idea that it is the character of our political leaders that determines the character of our democracy now appears somewhat quaint. More, perhaps, than in the past, we get the politicians we deserve.

This book begins with the story of a president who was partly responsible for what has been called 'the myth of the strong leader'. LBJ seemed to show that it was possible to get things done by sheer force of political will. All the other leaders I write about here have bought into that myth one way or another. But only one – the president I write about at the end – appears set on testing it to destruction. Trump makes leadership more important than ever, and also increasingly irrelevant. The paradox of populist leaders is that they promise to empower the people but end up accumulating more and more power in their own hands. They undermine the authority of the democratic offices they hold at the same time as exaggerating them. They are not probing the limits of their own power: they are testing the limits of democracy itself.

I do not know what comes next. Nor do I want to downplay the significant differences that exist between the US and British political systems. Presidents can still do things that prime ministers can't, and vice versa. The challenge of dealing with Congress remains quite distinct from the task of managing Parliament. Brexit, ultimately, is a very different phenomenon from the presidency of Trump, and Boris Johnson's premiership will likewise be very different again. (I write more about Johnson in the new afterword that can be found at the end of this book.) But if the result of the turmoil of the past few years is that we end up with less faith in the power of presidents and prime ministers to make all the difference, that will be no bad thing. Maybe what comes after the myth of the strong leader is the idea of leaderless democracy. There are far worse ideas.

When Margaret Thatcher, the closest Britain has had to a strong leader in modern times, died in 2013, many of her diehard critics celebrated on Twitter by announcing: 'Ding, Dong! The Witch is dead!' But it's not the return of the Wicked Witch we should fear. It's the revenge of the frustrated Wizard.

1

LYNDON JOHNSON

LYNDON JOHNSON ALWAYS BELIEVED he would be president. As a boy in Texas, growing up in poor and sometimes desperate circumstances, he told anyone who would listen that he was headed for the White House. He mapped out a plan to get there, from which, as his biographer Robert Caro writes, 'he refused to be diverted'. It meant first establishing himself in state politics, then winning a seat in the House of Representatives, then moving up to the Senate and finally on to the highest office of all. He was undaunted by the fact that no Southerner had been president for the best part of a century. In the view of many experts no Southerner could be elected president, because the numerically and economically superior Northern states would never stand for it. Johnson would prove the experts wrong.

In his early campaigns he insisted his managers refer to him by his three initials, as a mark of his future status. 'FDR–LBJ, FDR–LBJ,' he told them. 'Do you get it?' During the 1950s, when he was 'master of the Senate', and perhaps the most brilliant and ruthless political operator that body had ever seen, he refused to support any measure that might circumscribe presidential power, especially in foreign affairs. As Senate leader he would have benefited from the additional leverage over the White House this could have given him, but he wasn't interested in that: he would be president himself one day.

So it came to pass. As president, Johnson took advantage of all the powers of office he had done his best to preserve intact. These powers, along with his secretive and manipulative personality, allowed him to drag the country step by step into the Vietnam War. The oversight that might have saved him from his folly was not there. The war ultimately destroyed his presidency and much of his reputation. This, then, looks like a familiar story: the politician whose remarkable faith in his own abilities brought him to the top and then undid him once he got there. But Johnson's story does not quite fit that pattern. The reason is straightforward: his plan didn't work. In fact, it was an abject failure. LBJ didn't know how to make himself president, and his attempts to do so resulted only in humiliation and despair. It was an event over which he had no control – the assassination of JFK – that bridged the gap between his sense of his rightful position and his own capacity to achieve it. His destiny was to be a deeply disappointed man, until Lee Harvey Oswald intervened to redeem him. (I am assuming here that Johnson had nothing to do with the assassination, as does Caro, who says that in his many years of research he has found nothing to suggest any involvement in or foreknowledge of Kennedy's killing on Johnson's part. You may choose not to believe this. But if you don't believe it, you won't believe much else in this chapter, so it might be best to stop reading here.)

It is the mismatch between Johnson's fate prior to the assassination and his fate in its aftermath that gives the story of his rise to the presidency its compelling but also unfathomable flavour. The story really starts at the 1956 Democratic Convention, when Johnson made his first bid for the nomination. At that point he had firmly established himself as the dominant figure in the Senate, despite still being one of its younger members (he was forty-seven). He had proved a master manipulator of his fellow senators. His political gifts were perfectly suited to a small club of self-important men whom he could get at one on one. He alternately flattered them shamelessly and openly threatened them, never missing an opportunity to get them on the hook for something they either coveted or feared. Everyone knew that Johnson was the conduit through which their political ambitions must pass: he was the maker and breaker of legislation. In this way he made himself the most powerful Democratic politician in the country. He hoped that his standing would carry over into the nominating convention.

He knew he could not win the nomination with a direct appeal to the party, since too many people associated him with the Southern bloc in the Senate, which had been blocking civil rights legislation for more than fifty years. Johnson had always supported his fellow Southern senators in refusing to back anti-lynching legislation, claiming it was a matter for the individual states. This was the price he paid for getting them to do his bidding when he needed them. But it made him repugnant to the liberal wing of the party. To them, he reeked of 'magnolia'.

Nonetheless, Johnson believed that a brokered convention that could not coalesce around a liberal standard-bearer would turn to him as the man who delivered results: the supreme politician of the age. He was wrong. The party chose its liberal darling Adlai Stevenson for a second time, even though he stood little chance of defeating Eisenhower. Johnson received barely 5 per cent of the ballot. What surprised his supporters was not so much that he failed – it was hard to see how he could have succeeded, given his reputation – as that he failed to notice what was going on. He made a fool of himself, continuing to push his claims well past the point at which it was clear no one was listening. He had entirely misjudged what would be needed to get his way. His genius for manipulation had been no use to him: he had been manipulating the wrong people. Senators did not sway presidential nominations, state governors did, and Johnson had not cultivated them, partly because he had little he could tempt or threaten them with. He had almost no popular appeal, since he could not get his hands on the electorate one on one. He was out of his depth, and floundering.

Johnson tried to learn his lesson from this fiasco. He went back to the Senate determined to get a civil rights bill passed, and to be seen as the man – the only man – who could do it. It had to have his name on it. When, in 1957, the Civil Rights Bill finally made it out of the Senate, overcoming the longest filibuster in history to get there, Johnson was probably right to believe that he was the only man who could have pulled it off. In the end, the bill itself was so watered down that to many liberals it looked more like a defeat than a victory: all mention of desegregation was dropped in favour of an exclusive focus on black voting rights. These were to be enforced by jury trial, which is what made the legislation palatable to the Southern senators: they knew no Southern jury would convict an election official for failing to register black voters. Still, Johnson justified the bill in three ways. First, he had shown that civil rights legislation could get past the Senate: as he put it (with typical bluntness), once you lose your virginity there's nothing to stop you doing it again. Second, he claimed that voting rights were the key: once black voters were able to exercise some leverage at the ballot box, the rest would follow. Those were the public justifications. The private one was that Johnson could now present himself to the Democratic Party in 1960 as a plausible presidential candidate.

||||
||||

Once again, however, he got it wrong. What now stood in his way was not so much his public record as his private fears. He could see that in 1956 he'd been grabbing at something that was way beyond his reach. The consequence had been humiliation, the thing that Johnson was most afraid of throughout his life. His ruthless ambition was shaped by his resolve to be nothing like his father, a successful local politician whose wishful schemes and careless self-regard had ultimately plunged his family into poverty. When LBJ was a child, the Johnsons had become a laughing stock in their own town, Johnson City. He was determined that he would never be laughed at as a politician: if he reached for something he would have the weapons at his disposal to make sure he got it. When orchestrating votes in the Senate, he liked to win by a wide margin: the world had to see that he couldn't be beaten. In the words of one of his aides: 'He had a horror of defeat. An absolute horror of it.'

Though he was well placed to run in 1960, he couldn't be seen to run unless he could be sure he wouldn't be humiliated again. So he held back, refused to campaign in any of the primaries, denied that he was a candidate to any journalist who asked and refused to meet the governors whose support he would need at the convention. He agreed to give speeches that would have raised his profile as a candidate and then, at the last minute, cancelled them. The problem was that he already had a national profile as one of the most driven, ambitious men in the US. No one believed his protestations that he was happy to stay in the Senate, 'tending the store', as he put it. They thought he was running scared. The more he insisted he didn't want to be president, the more he was in danger of becoming a laughing stock. 'Fear of humiliation,' Caro writes, 'led to humiliation.'

Eventually, as the convention approached, he realised he could no longer hold back. He let it be known that he was a candidate and threw himself into the campaign. But by now it was too late. Once again he was hoping for a brokered convention, where he would emerge as the choice of the dealmakers. But John F. Kennedy, who had been risking his campaign in a series of hard-fought primary battles against the popular liberal Hubert Humphrey, had already tied up the votes he needed. Kennedy won on the first ballot, with more than half the delegates and twice as many as Johnson. It was better than 1956, but still nowhere near good enough. Kennedy had another advantage that Johnson couldn't match. American politics had entered the TV age, and Kennedy was the most telegenic person in American public life. It turned out you could after all get to the voters one on one, but not the Johnson way, with snarls and finger-wagging gestures. What it took was a boyish smile.

The day after he secured the nomination, Kennedy asked Johnson to be his running mate. This surprising decision remains shrouded in mystery. The received Kennedy myth, propagated years later, after Johnson had been seen to tarnish and then squander Camelot's golden legacy, was that JFK must have made the offer pro forma, in the clear expectation that LBJ would turn it down. Why would a man who had the Senate in the palm of his hand trade all that power for an office that was, in the famous words of one of its previous occupants, 'not worth a pitcher of warm piss'? But both men probably knew what they were about: Kennedy wanted Johnson because of what he could bring to the ticket, and because he would be much less trouble inside the White House than ruling the roost in the Senate; Johnson wanted to run because he saw all other routes to the White House being closed off to him. The person who could not understand it was Robert Kennedy, who had hated Johnson from the moment he set eyes on him ten years earlier, when Bobby was a young staffer and LBJ was lording it over the Senate. Bobby desperately tried to persuade his brother that it was a mistake to bring into the fold a man he considered a monster. When that failed, he went to Johnson himself to try to talk him out of it. All he succeeded in doing was securing his lifelong enmity.

We can be confident JFK was serious, because he went to the trouble of persuading Johnson's mentor Sam Rayburn, the veteran Texan speaker of the House, to let his man run. Rayburn was adamantly opposed to the idea after what he'd seen happen to another Texan titan, John Nance Garner, who had traded his power as speaker of the House to become FDR's running mate in 1932. Eight years later Garner went back to Texas a bitter man, to eke out his days as a pecan farmer; the vice-presidency had broken him. (It was Garner who compared the office to a pitcher of piss.) Rayburn thought Johnson would be making the same mistake, but Kennedy and Johnson between them talked him round. We know Johnson was serious, because he asked his aides to find out the statistics on vice-presidential successions. How many presidents had died in office? The answer was seven out of thirty-three. Johnson liked the odds: better than one in five.

||||
||||

This is the part of the story that looks creepiest, in the light of what was to come. Here is Johnson the implacable man of destiny spotting another route to the top, this one spattered with blood. But once again, he probably miscalculated. Johnson was preoccupied with Kennedy's health. He rightly suspected it was much worse than the youthful-looking candidate was letting on. Kennedy was suffering from Addison's disease, which, undiagnosed, had nearly killed him as a young man, though cortisone injections eventually gave him a new lease of life. One of the reasons Johnson had persistently underestimated Kennedy was that he thought he was simply too sickly to be president. 'Yella, yella' was the way he used to describe the young senator, meaning not that he was a coward (like all the Kennedys, JFK was physically absurdly brave) but that he was jaundiced and gaunt. As it turned out, the 'yella' Kennedy looked golden on TV, whereas the large, heavy Johnson usually appeared uncomfortable on the small screen: too big for the little box in the corner. Johnson must have suspected that Kennedy's health would break down over the course of eight years in the White House. He was also conscious that his own health might not last long enough for him to fight a fresh battle for the presidency in 1968. He had

had a massive heart attack in 1955, and he knew the men in his family tended not to live beyond their early sixties. Johnson was almost certainly thinking not of the assassin's bullet when he weighed the odds, but of the race between the two men to beat the surgeon's knife.

Kennedy was confident that his health would hold. Certainly he liked his chances against Johnson. 'I am forty-three years old,' he told aides who worried that LBJ as vice-president would be a hostage to fortune, 'and I'm the healthiest candidate for president in the United States.' He also liked his chances with Johnson on the ticket. Kennedy had calculated that the attributes that made Johnson unacceptable to the Democratic Party as a presidential candidate – his Southern roots, his crude politicking – would serve him well as a running mate. He was right about that.

Johnson's skills were well suited to campaigning for vice-president. He didn't have to debate his opponents or set out a vision for the country. He simply had to tour the South in his own thirteen-carriage train – the 'LBJ Special' – glad-handing local dignitaries and feeding the crowds his inimitable no-nonsense hokum. His speeches were short, sentimental and to the point. 'What has Dick Nixon ever done for you?' he would ask in each small town, and he would smile and wave and wax lyrical about his Southern childhood, poverty and all. He also found opportunities to exercise the darker side of his political personality. In Florida he met in private with a group of state Democratic leaders who he felt had been lukewarm in getting behind the campaign. 'This boy Kennedy is going to win and he's going to win big,' he told them. 'And if he wins without the South, I'm warning you – I'm warning you – you bastards are going to be dead. You'll get nothing out of the Kennedy administration.' After that, the Washington muckraker Drew Pearson noted, Florida's top Democrats 'really began to work'.

Finally, Johnson brought to the ticket his well-honed skills in vote-rigging (the vital skill being not so much the rigging

as the getting away with it). Johnson's first and most important job was to deliver his home state to Kennedy. He was
not as popular in Texas as he had been, and his attempts to
position himself for a national campaign had alienated local
conservative Democrats, who saw themselves being sold out
to the liberals. For many, Johnson's decision to run alongside
Kennedy, an archetypal Northern liberal snob, was the final
straw. But Johnson knew how to win in Texas without being
popular. He had first captured his Senate seat in 1948 in an
incredibly close contest – he won by just 87 votes – thanks
to some ballot-stuffing that had been brazen even by Texan
standards. Ballot boxes, particularly in poor Mexican districts,
that delivered for Johnson by implausible margins in 1948 did
the same again in 1960. The notorious Precinct 13, which in
1948 produced 202 ballots for Johnson certified in the names
of voters who were dead on election day, went for the Democratic ticket in 1960 by a margin of 1,144 to 45. The pattern was
repeated across the poorer parts of the state. Kennedy won
Texas; he won the South; and he won the presidency.

But if Kennedy got what he wanted from the election,
Johnson didn't. His hope had been that he would be a different
kind of vice-president from his predecessors because he had a
better understanding of power than they did. 'Power is where
power goes,' was his motto. He was the most powerful man
in the Senate, and he was moving, so the power would move
with him. It is true that some vice-presidents have been much
more powerful than others (for example, Dick Cheney). But
it only happens when the president decides to let it happen
(for example, George W. Bush). No one can bring power to
the office by their own efforts. Johnson tried in the early days,
throwing his weight around in the Democratic caucus in the
Senate as though nothing had changed. He was politely, and
then less politely, ignored. He discovered he had no political
weapons to threaten anyone with; all he had was the authority
of the president he served. His personal authority was gone.

Kennedy, having got what he wanted out of Johnson, had no intention of giving him any leverage over the direction of his administration. He knew full well the kind of man Johnson was: a politician of vast ambition and extraordinary touchiness. This meant he would have to butter him up to shut him up. He told one of his staffers: 'You are dealing with a very insecure, sensitive man with a huge ego. I want you literally to kiss his fanny from one end of Washington to the other.' No one was to ignore Johnson; at the same time, no one was to listen to him. Johnson could have helped the administration in one crucial respect: he knew better than anyone how to get legislation through Congress. But Kennedy had no wish to draw on these skills, for fear that people would say it was Johnson who was pulling the strings. So Johnson languished in the doldrums, cosseted but wholly ineffective; and so, for the most part, did Kennedy's legislative programme.

When he realised that vice-presidents couldn't get their way by menace, Johnson resorted to the only other reliable weapon in his armoury: shameless flattery. As his power waned, he became more and more subservient to the president, doing whatever he was bid, touring the world on endless goodwill trips, never uttering a word against his boss (though he continued to seethe against Bobby). When asked, he said he was happier than he had ever been, and that Kennedy was the best president he could imagine. In cabinet meetings this most loquacious of men sat silently and merely nodded assent. All he could see to do was hang in there, and hope against hope that his time would come. Once again, he became a laughing stock. The Kennedys' Washington – a town of intellectuals, sophisticates and creeps, good-time boys and party girls with a taste for the jugular – mocked Johnson's corniness and his down-home style (pronouncing 'hors d'oeuvres' as 'whores doves' at an official reception), but what they were really doing was revelling in his thwarted ambitions. By now Johnson knew he was being humiliated. 'WHATEVER HAPPENED TO

LBJ?' became a regular newspaper headline and a running joke.

Even here, by choosing to suck it up, he may have miscalculated. By the second half of 1963, people in the know were beginning to ask whether Kennedy would drop Johnson from the ticket the following year, which would have been the death of his political ambitions. Kennedy always denied it, and there is no evidence that he ever discussed the possibility with his advisers. But this hardly settles the matter. Kennedy had shown himself Johnson's equal in ruthlessness, and he was quite capable of deciding these things for himself (he had, after all, barely discussed his decision to put Johnson on the ticket in 1960, even with his brother). By 1963 it was no longer clear what Johnson had to offer: his subservience to the president had made him so unpopular in Texas that it was uncertain whether even the dark arts could rescue him there. Worse, he was now becoming a target for scandal.

Life magazine was preparing to run a story on his personal fortune, which was built on the ownership of media outlets in Texas through which political favours were routinely traded for advertising revenue. At the same time one of his former aides, Bobby Baker, was under Senate investigation as part of a money, spies and call girls scandal that had uncomfortable echoes of the Profumo affair in Britain, which brought down a prime minister. On 22 November 1963 Johnson found himself in Texas as part of a long-delayed fundraising trip with the president, which had given Kennedy a chance to see for himself how little clout Johnson now carried in his home state. On the same day, in Washington, the Senate Rules Committee was interviewing Don Reynolds, the man who had signed the cheques that provided the link between the Baker scandal and Johnson's business affairs. Meanwhile, in New York, *Life* was planning to carry the story about LBJ's finances in its next issue. The stag was at bay.

Then, of course, everything changed in an instant. Caro's riveting account of the day of the assassination, which was extracted in the *New Yorker* as though it were a short story in its own right – which, in a way, it is – represents a pivotal moment not just in the arc of Johnson's life but in the modern history of political biography. What might have seemed familiar becomes startlingly fresh, because we get to see it from the perspective of the man whose destiny suddenly came back into focus as the world of those around him was falling apart. The chaos of the event stands in obvious contrast to Johnson's preternatural calm as it was unfolding. Indeed, so calm and focused was he, and so coolly efficient in taking command, that it is almost as though he had been expecting it.

This is what gives nourishment to the conspiracy theorists: the idea that no one could be so alive to the possibilities in the moment who did not know of them in advance. But what really comes across is Johnson's instant recognition that his political fortunes were back in his own hands. It was his personality that was asserting itself, not his prior knowledge. He was calm because he had genuine choices to make, for the first time in years. Johnson's political persona was that of a 'decider': politics only made sense to him when he could impose his will on a situation. Now, at last, he could. And he did.

Some of his decisions were wholly rational. In the hours after Kennedy's death he spent time pleading with the administration's shell-shocked senior officials to stay in their posts, saying that he needed them more than their former boss ever had. He was, as always, shameless in his use of wheedling flattery. He was just poor ol' Lyndon, he told them, a man without any of Kennedy's intellectual gifts and charismatic authority. He would be lost without their guidance. They were the brightest and the best: they had to help him, for the sake of the country. Almost all of them did. Some of his decisions were extraordinarily callous. Within minutes of the death being confirmed he called up Bobby Kennedy, not to offer words of comfort or consolation but to ask him as attorney general for the correct form of words for the oath of office that he was about to swear on Air Force One. Bobby never forgave him, though given that Johnson knew Bobby would never forgive him anyway, that was presumably the point: to remind the younger brother that implacable hatred was no barrier to a fundamental shift of power between them.

And some of his decisions were simply breathtaking in their ruthless self-assertion. One reason Johnson wanted to be sworn in on the tarmac in Dallas rather than waiting until he was back in Washington was that he had a judge in mind to perform the task. Her name was Sarah Hughes, a long-time Johnson ally from Dallas whom he had nominated as a federal district judge in 1961, at the start of his vice-presidency. As a Texas appointment he had assumed this was in his gift. But the Justice Department (Bobby's fiefdom) had told him that at sixty-four Hughes was too old for an administration that wanted to get younger judges on the federal bench. Johnson was outraged, but agreed to offer the position to another Texas lawyer. Then Bobby discovered that Sam Rayburn also wanted to see Hughes get the job and that he was prepared to hold up important legislation in the House until she did. The Justice Department immediately changed its tune and announced her appointment the next day. Now Johnson felt humiliated. It was the first and perhaps the bluntest indication that in becoming vice-president he had given up his ability to get his way. He was powerless, which was the thing he most hated being. Nearly three years later, and within minutes of learning that he was to be president, he acted to undo this humiliation.

In the famous photo of Johnson taking the oath in the crowded aircraft cabin, his hand raised and his face as sombre as it is possible to imagine, with his wife, Lady Bird, on one side and Kennedy's widow, Jackie, still in her blood-stained coat, on the other, the tiny figure in front holding the Bible is Sarah Hughes. Johnson choreographed every aspect of the picture. It sent out all the signals he wanted to convey: continuity, dignity, grief, humility and, for the very few people who would understand, revenge.

In the days that followed, the pattern repeated itself. Johnson was calm, self-controlled and utterly decisive. He recognised at once that the way to assert and entrench his power was not to break with JFK's presidency but to be seen to complete it. Johnson's position after the assassination was highly precarious. Loathed by most of the former president's men, mistrusted and derided by the Washington establishment, increasingly forgotten by the American people, he was taking office less than a year before the next presidential election. That election would be his opportunity – his only opportunity – to legitimise his presidency, yet he could not be seen to electioneer in the aftermath of the assassination: it would have been grotesque. Johnson's fear – his fear throughout his presidency – was that Bobby would emerge to reclaim the crown from the usurper in the name of his brother. At the same time, Johnson took office at a very dangerous moment in the life of the nation. The Cold War was still at its height, dark theories of Cuban or Russian involvement in the assassination were widespread and the country was rife with social, and particularly racial, tensions (in part because of Kennedy's failure to make significant progress on civil rights legislation, which was still being stymied in the Senate). A misstep could have proved disastrous not just for Johnson's presidency but for the wider world.

||||
||||

The US was lucky to have a man like Johnson in charge at this treacherous moment. Few people could have coped as he did. It is easy to imagine other politicians, no matter how experienced, being overwhelmed by the responsibility or intimidated by the risks. But it should be said that Johnson too was very lucky: the situation suited him perfectly. He had no need to fear humiliation: the country was too shaken and grief-stricken to pay much attention to what he did. (The assassination also had the magical effect of making the Baker scandal and the investigation into Johnson's finances go away, at least until they could no longer do him terminal damage.) He knew he couldn't compete with the tragic glamour of the bereaved Kennedys, and he didn't try. He stayed in the background during the days of official mourning, behaving more like a funeral director than one of the mourners-in-chief. He did his real work behind the scenes, where he knew he could be most effective.

He was able to concentrate on domestic affairs because the international situation remained quiet. The Russians, probably no less alarmed by the conspiracy theories than anyone else, were careful to do nothing to raise tensions. Johnson addressed the American public's desire to know the truth by quickly setting up the Warren Commission to investigate the assassination. He had been spared the worst of the public's suspicions of his own motives by another piece of good fortune: his closest Texan ally, Governor John Connally, who had been travelling with Kennedy in the motorcade, had also taken a bullet (he survived). If the president was going to be shot in Texas, then it was essential for Johnson's reputation that a Texan should take a hit too. (Lady Bird, who emerges from the story as a remarkably selfless woman, also recognised this: 'I only wish it could have been me,' she said.) Getting the right people onto the Warren Commission offered a masterclass in doing politics the LBJ way. He wanted another of his mentors, the Georgia senator Richard Russell, to serve as his eyes and ears on the committee. Russell refused: he was too old, he said, and ill (he had emphysema); in fact, he hated the idea of working under Earl Warren, the Republican chief justice and a man he despised. So Johnson got to work on Russell, begging him, pleading with him and ultimately abasing himself before him. 'I haven't got any daddy,' he told the old man, 'and you are going to be it.' While this was still going on, Johnson announced to the press that Russell had agreed to serve. So he also told him that any backsliding now would look to the world like an unpatriotic betrayal of his duty. He would hang Russell out to dry. 'Daddy' eventually did what he was asked.

But the arena in which Johnson showed his true mastery was the one where he had always been king: Congress. Again, the situation was set up perfectly for him. He had two imperatives: to honour the memory of his predecessor, and to demonstrate that he was his own man. The way to achieve both was to show that he would not simply get Kennedy's domestic programme passed: he would surpass it. He would give JFK his legacy by pushing a liberal agenda far more ambitious than any that had been proposed before, encompassing a war on poverty, wide-ranging civil rights legislation and tax reform. Kennedy's programme was stuck in Congress, in part because Kennedy had refused to use Johnson's expertise in negotiating the minutiae of the legislative process. In his first State of the Union address Johnson told Congress that they must now take that programme forward and complete it. He announced this in a spirit of continuity and reverence for the fallen hero. But were he to succeed, he would be sending a different message: the only way to pass Kennedy's programme was to have a Johnson presidency. He was doing what the man who beat him in 1960 couldn't have done.

He began by dismissing his previous reputation as a Southern conservative. He sent out a message to the liberals in his own party, telling them: 'I am a Roosevelt New Dealer [...] I'm no budget slasher [...] To tell the truth, JFK was a little too conservative to suit my tastes.' But he knew that the liberals were not his real problem. He had to get past his old Southern allies. Kennedy's true failing, as he saw it, was not his conservatism but his lack of attention to detail. Kennedy had assumed he could outflank the conservative wing of his party by relying on the rising tide of national public opinion. But the US was (and still is) a federal state. The Southern senators were impervious to the tide of national opinion: they were answerable to their home state electorates, which continued to reward them for blocking change by voting them back into office. Johnson saw that they couldn't be outflanked; they would have to be accommodated instead. He also saw that the only way to win was to deprive the Southern bloc of its most effective weapon, which was delay. The time-honoured tactic of the South was to create a logjam whenever civil rights legislation was on the table: an administration that tried to force it through would find that there was no time for anything else, even passing a budget. Faced with that prospect, everyone, including the liberals, invariably backed down. Johnson decided to break the logjam by getting the budget through first. And that meant giving the Southern conservatives the sort of budget they wanted: a balanced one. Johnson spotted the thing that had eluded the best and brightest around Kennedy: the only way to pass a liberal agenda was to be a budget slasher.

At the end of 1963 the man sitting on top of the logjam was Harry Byrd, a seventy-six-year-old senator from Virginia and the Democratic chair of the Senate Finance Committee. Byrd was a classic Southern conservative: a self-styled man of honour and unabashed racist, he feared only one thing more than the intermingling of the races, and that was loose public finance. If Johnson had a horror of defeat, Byrd had a horror of debt. He had an 'extreme obsessive hatred' of it, a 'fixation on frugality' born of his struggles as a fifteen-year-old to rescue his father's nickel-and-dime newspaper business. Now, sixty years on, Byrd was adamant that the federal budget should not exceed the symbolic figure of $100 billion. That meant substantial cuts. The Kennedy administration had not managed to find them. Johnson understood that Byrd would not move without them. He would simply sit on the tax bill in his committee, holding everything up. So Johnson decided to give Byrd his budget cuts. But, in classic Johnson fashion, he made his point by going further. By relentlessly badgering his officials, and refusing to listen to their excuses, he got the budget down to $97.9 billion. Then he called Byrd into the White House and told him: 'I got the damn thing down under one hundred billion – way under. Now you can tell your friends that you forced the president of the United States to reduce the budget before you let him have his tax cut.' After that, Byrd moved, and so did the entire legislative programme.

Johnson's great achievements – the civil rights and social welfare legislation that formed his 'Great Society' programme – came later in 1964 and then, after his overwhelming election victory in November, during the early years of his 'legitimate' presidency. To get this legislation through he had to take on the Southern Democrats, break their filibuster in the Senate and put together a coalition of Northern and Western senators. In parting ways so decisively with his former colleagues, he reshaped American politics. But these victories were only made possible by what he did in the hours, days, weeks and months following the assassination, when he established beyond doubt that he was, contrary to everything his detractors had always feared, up to the job of being president. He understood what needed to be done, for his own sake and the country's, and he knew how to do it. He remained calm and he didn't overreach himself. But he did reach for the limit of what was possible, determined not to squander his opportunity. No longer fearing humiliation, he was able to avoid it entirely. By April 1964, his approval rating stood at 77 per cent. More surprisingly, for someone who had once been seen as far too divisive a figure to be president, only 9 per cent of Americans disapproved of the job he was doing.

||||
||||

It is an inspiring story. Yet as one reads about it, it is hard not to be haunted by the sense of an alternative destiny. Some of this concerns the what-ifs surrounding the assassination itself: what if the bullets had missed Kennedy, leaving Johnson to face his hapless fate, his career running out of road, his reputation on the brink of ruin? He would still have had his achievements as master of the Senate, but that is unlikely to have been enough, either for him or for future historians. As a failed vice-president he would be counted a failure, insofar as he would be remembered at all. It seems highly improbable that Caro would have thought it worth devoting half his own life to writing the life of such a man. Among the accidents of biography are the accidents of whose lives get written: all presidents and prime ministers get one, regardless of merit; far fewer vice-presidents do. Johnson's luck includes the fact that his later good fortune is what gave his earlier achievements the attention they deserve. He has become the role model for a later generation of politicians not just because he was so good at politics but also because what made him good at politics found its way into the light through no merit of his own. That thought, however, leads to another one: what made Johnson good at politics was also what made him bad at politics, when the occasion wasn't right. So what might have happened if Johnson had mastered his destiny in the way he always imagined? What if he had somehow conquered his demons and seized the nomination in 1960, through some alternative piece of good fortune? What if he had been in charge, not during the fraught days of late November 1963, but during the even more fraught days of late October 1962?

This is the truly sobering alternative reality. Johnson, so perfectly suited to his moment after the assassination, was almost the last person anyone would have wanted in charge a year earlier, as the world faced its possible Armageddon during the Cuban missile crisis. As vice-president, he was present throughout as the crisis was unfolding, yet he remained just a bystander. He sat in on the big meetings, but JFK, RFK and the small group of men they trusted had no intention of seeking

his advice, let alone taking it. All the key decisions were made
without him, and he wasn't even told about the final, precarious trade with Khrushchev (in which Kennedy pledged not to
invade Cuba and hinted at the withdrawal of American mis-
siles from Turkey if the Russians would dismantle their bases
in Cuba). Yet there are moments when we get a glimpse of
what it might have been like if Johnson had been in the top
job. He was a hawk because, as always, the thing he feared was
humiliation. He saw the Russian threat as being to American
prestige and any concessions as ones that would embolden a
bully. During one meeting of ExComm, the top-level group
assembled to advise the president during the crisis, Johnson
took advantage of the fact that both Kennedy brothers were
out of the room to let the assembled company know what he
thought: 'All I know is that when I was a boy in Texas, and you
were walking along the road, when a rattlesnake reared up
ready to strike, the only thing to do was take a stick and chop
its head off.' Caro writes: 'There was a little chill in the room
after that statement.' Then Bobby came back in and Johnson
shut up again.

When the crisis was over, both Kennedys were confirmed
in their view that Johnson must never become president. They
had been appalled by the glimpses they'd been given of his
recklessness and his bravado, but also by his cravenness and
his passivity: his ideas were crass and foolish, but he lacked the
courage even to defend them to their faces. It is impossible to
know what might have happened had Johnson been in charge.
Probably the outcome would have been far worse. But perhaps
Khrushchev would not have pushed his own luck so far, had
he known that a man like Johnson had his hand on the nuclear
button. In fact, the person Johnson most resembles in this crisis
is Khrushchev himself. Both men – older, rougher, politically
battle-hardened, masters of the politics of manipulation – had
consistently underestimated Kennedy, whom they viewed as
inexperienced and soft. In the end Kennedy outmanoeuvred

both of them: he was much tougher and smarter than they had imagined. Khrushchev's fate in 1964, turfed out of office and left to live out his days bitter and disappointed, is a glimpse of what Johnson's might have been had Kennedy lived.

This thought, though, suggests one more what-if: what might a man of Johnson's political temperament have been capable of under another political system, one that gave a freer rein to the dark side of his personality? Johnson was a tyrant by nature. He bullied the people around him, treated them with contempt when it suited him and had little regard for their sensitivities or feelings. He was cruel, capricious, devious, brutal and often terrifying. He was also, when it suited him, sentimental, generous and capable of compassion on a grand scale. It is, perhaps, easier to imagine him reaching the top by his own efforts under the Soviet system than under the American one. It is also fairly easy to imagine what terrible things he might have done when he got there.

||||
||||

Caro's thesis, which he repeats across the volumes of his epic and still unfinished biography, is that although power always corrupts, 'what is seldom said, but what is equally true, is that power always *reveals*'. The more power someone has, the easier it is to see the true person behind the mask. When politicians get to make the really big choices for themselves, then we get to see who they really are. This strikes me as entirely the wrong way round. Power doesn't tell us the true nature of the man; the man tells us the true nature of the power. Caro wants us to see that when Johnson had the big choices to make in late 1963 and early 1964, the real Johnson, who had been obscured for decades on his path to the top, came to the surface. This man was not just the 'decider' but someone who would decide for justice, and who became, in Caro's words, 'the codifier of compassion'. Johnson, he says, had always cared deeply about the injustice being done to blacks, to Mexicans, to the poor and downtrodden, but had never had the chance to show how much he cared. When he got that chance, he took it.

Yet the reason he took it was not because he cared but because it was the way to assert himself, given the kind of power he inherited. It was his way of outdoing his predecessor, outflanking his rivals and imposing himself and his will on the American system of government, with all its checks and balances, its quirks and prejudices. Compassion wasn't the purpose of power for Johnson. In these circumstances compassion *was* power, a means and not an end. Perhaps the person who saw this best is the other dominant political figure of the age, someone who probably understood Johnson better than Kennedy did. Martin Luther King told his supporters, who were fearful of what a Texan like Johnson would do in the White House: 'LBJ is a man of great ego and great power. He is a pragmatist and a man of pragmatic compassion. It may just be that he's going to go where John Kennedy couldn't.' Ego came before power, power came before pragmatism, pragmatism came before compassion. Johnson would always use whatever weapons were at hand to dominate. It was lucky for America's poor and oppressed that in late 1963, in the extraordinary circumstances in which he found himself, the most useful weapon at hand was social justice.

The truth is that when we finally get to see Johnson with the power he always craved, the real man behind the mask becomes if anything even harder to identify. There is an unknowable quality to him as he approached and then reached the summit of American political life. From 1960 to 1963 Johnson was cowed and craven; then from 1963 to 1964 he was self-controlled and dominant. Yet along the way there are grim mutterings from those around him about another Johnson: the blood-sucking monster. Ralph Dungan, JFK's special assistant, said of Johnson: 'He really took the substance, the psychological and spiritual substance of people and sucked it right out like a vampire [...] He could not leave a man whole with his own dignity and his own self-esteem.' Bobby Kennedy called him 'mean, bitter, vicious, an animal in many ways'. These might sound like the ravings of paranoid and disappointed men, were it not for what we know of Johnson before 1960, when he often did appear in this light. Johnson abused his subordinates, especially the women, and including the blacks. He was an equal opportunity employer in that he seems to have been willing to mistreat anyone who was beneath him, just as he was willing to ingratiate himself to anyone who had power over him. His compassion did not very often extend to his own family, or to his wife or daughters, whom he routinely neglected and sometimes humiliated.

There is little of that in the heroic story of Johnson's early presidency, yet we do still get the occasional flash of casual cruelty. In late 1963 the newly sworn-in Johnson held court at his ranch in Texas, where he invited West Germany's new chancellor, Ludwig Erhard, for a state visit. It was a triumphant success. The Washington press corps, which had spent the previous years mocking Johnson's down-home corniness, now revelled in it (it's amazing what proximity to power will do to journalists as well). Johnson was relaxed and welcoming, holding informal press conferences on his front lawn. One of these took place on Christmas Day, when Johnson introduced all twenty-seven members of his extended family who had come for Christmas dinner. These included his two daughters, Lucy and Lynda. 'Lynda was wearing her Christmas gift from her father,' Caro writes, 'a loose-fitting red shift; [Johnson] reached out and bundled up the fabric, to prove, he said with a smile, that she wasn't in a family way.' Lynda was nineteen at the time. How the journalists must have laughed.

While he was charming the press corps that Christmas, the new president was also turning the screws on their bosses. Johnson was determined to get the Texas newspapers that had criticised him in the past to come back on board. He wanted their pledges to support him put in writing. And if they didn't deliver, he warned them that he would use his power as president to ruin them. He told the publishers of the *Houston Chronicle* that he required a signed letter promising to support him so long as he remained in office. If he didn't get that letter, he would block a planned bank merger that the owners of the newspaper were depending on. Johnson's advisers warned him that now he was president this sort of brazen horse-trading might not be wise. Did he really have to get the *quid pro quo* in writing? Yes, Johnson said, he did. And anyway, the letter need only specify the *quo*, not the *quid:* the promise of support, not the reward. But without it, the bank deal was off. Johnson got his letter. He locked it in a drawer. And the *Houston Chronicle* never wavered in its support throughout his presidency, even as it eventually fell apart over Vietnam.

Who is to say which was the real Johnson? Was it the man of compassion or the secretive bully? If and when Caro completes his tale, we will eventually get to hear how Johnson's secretiveness, his horror of defeat ('I am not going to lose Vietnam,' he told Kennedy's foreign affairs team two days after the assassination, 'I am not going to be the president who saw South-East Asia go the way China went') and his obsession with outdoing the Kennedys caught up with him in the end. His doing will eventually be his undoing, as it so often is. Will this get us closer to the heart of the man? I don't think so. In history, as in fiction, the story is all.

As I was reading about Johnson's rise to the presidency, I also found myself reading Hilary Mantel's *Bring Up the Bodies*, the second volume of her fictionalised life of Thomas Cromwell. Some critics have complained of Mantel's book that it does not get us any closer to the true Thomas Cromwell than its predecessor, *Wolf Hall*. Instead, he becomes more opaque and unknowable as his power increases. But this is the essential truth. Power does not reveal. If anything, it fractures the human personality, as it passes through the prism of moments of choice. Mantel's Cromwell reminded me of Caro's Johnson, or perhaps it was the other way round. Reading about these great, brutal, terrifying men in intimate detail, one sees how big a part happenstance plays in their stories. Men like this know how to use their luck. But their luck is also using them.

2

MARGARET THATCHER

IT CAN BE DEPRESSING to discover that political fortune favours the people who keep going longest. But it does. That is one of the clear lessons from the life and career of Margaret Thatcher. It is not simply because of the longevity of her time in office: the eleven years and 209 days she spent at the top make her the longest-serving British prime minister of the twentieth century. It also comes through in the story of how she got there. She was not more intelligent than her rivals, or more principled. She chopped and changed as much as they did. But she was a lot more relentless: if anything, she kept chopping and changing long after they had given up and gone home. She didn't outsmart or outperform her enemies. She outstayed them.

A lot has sometimes been made of Thatcher's physical stamina – above all, her ability to function on four hours' sleep a night. This is something of a myth, part of the endless mythologising that surrounds her. It is true that she didn't sleep much, but often this made her tetchy and erratic. The people who worked for her knew when she was tired, and they also knew when to use 'tiredness' as a euphemism for her having had one whisky too many. Her authorised biographer Charles Moore is quite coy on this subject, never telling us exactly how much she drank. She consumed plentiful quantities of whisky and ginger ale, 'but she was never drunk', and she did not get through as much as her husband, Denis, who could more or less subsist on gin. She didn't have hangovers, and she didn't get ill (she sometimes had toothache). Her skin continued to glow, and her eye remained fierce. More striking than the amount of sleep she needed was her ability to sleep at all, given what she put herself and others through on a daily basis. She had no hobbies and no real interests outside politics, though she did occasionally indulge in bouts of housework as a way to pass the time. What she really liked to do was worry away at political problems. She was a stickler for detail and a devoted consumer of her red boxes of official documents. When things went wrong for her, she invariably concluded it was because she had been insufficiently prepared, and resolved to get back to her papers. Time and again she surprised many of those she met – from heads of state to humble journalists – by how well she was briefed.

It was partly a result of her upbringing ('We were Methodist,' she liked to say of her Grantham childhood, 'and Methodist means method') and partly down to her training as a chemist at Oxford – she was much more proud of being the first prime minister with a science degree than she was of being the first woman prime minister – and then as a barrister. But it was also a matter of temperament. She liked to badger people, picking away at the same few threads until something started to give. Moore writes of her governing style: 'She used every remark, every memo, every meeting as an opportunity to challenge existing habits, criticise any sign of ignorance, confusion or waste and preach incessantly the main aims of her administration.' Unsurprisingly, this made her tiring to be around. Five days after she became prime minister in 1979 she got her private secretary to let the Foreign Office know that she was disappointed with the briefing documents they had so far produced for her. 'She hopes that in future Departments will avoid wordy generalisations and the re-statement of facts

or conclusions which are, or should be, well known to all those
for whom the briefs are designed. The prime minister, who is a
quick reader, is fully prepared to tackle long briefs when necessary: but she would like their content to be pithy and concisely
expressed.' Longer but pithier: it's a good summary of her
draining, rat-a-tat-a-tat-a-tat-a-tat approach to politics. A few
intimates came to adore her for being so impossible to work
with; the longer they survived the ordeal, the more closely
they bonded with each other. But most people were worn out.

   A recurring theme in the tributes that followed her death
in 2013 was the difference between her brutal handling of her
colleagues and her solicitous treatment of juniors and under-
lings. But really these were the two sides of a single personality
trait: the relentlessness of her acts of kindness could be hard to
distinguish from the relentlessness of her acts of aggression.
'It was a great mistake to tell the prime minister that one of
your children had got measles or something, because she'd go
on talking about it for some days afterwards,' one member of
her Downing Street staff complained. 'She could carry this to
really quite absurd lengths for a prime minister.' Moore writes:
'Despite the fact that Mrs Thatcher was an egotist, she was also
almost always extremely considerate towards staff and their
families.' That 'despite' should be a 'because of'. The woman
who was constantly trying to help people out of their personal difficulties – offering to cook them meals, sending them
flowers, showering them with concern – was recognisably the
same person of whom Jim Prior complained to Hugo Young
in 1981: 'She hasn't really got a friend left in the whole cabinet.
One reason she has no friend is that she subjects everyone to
the most emotionally exhausting arguments; the other is that
she still interrupts everyone all the time. It makes us all absolutely furious.' Her modus operandi, in private life as in public,
was to go on and on and on.

   This tenacity was visible from the outset of her career,
and it was the thing that set her apart. The bare story of her

political ascent is astonishing – a grocer's daughter from the middle of England (which in High Tory terms might as well have been the middle of nowhere), blessed with moderate gifts, plump, prettyish, quite bright, no real connections, full of pluck but lacking in guile, who winds up as prime minister and the dominant political figure of the age – but it rarely seems astonishing as it unfolds. Her progress, for all its ostensible improbability, was remarkably smooth. There were few sudden shifts in her fortunes. Instead, she knocks on each successive door, and though it doesn't always open straight away, she keeps knocking and eventually it does open. Already, in her early twenties, she was being spoken of as a future prime minister. She was selected as the Conservative parliamentary candidate for Dartford at the age of twenty-three, standing in both the 1950 and 1951 general elections. She stood out from other prospective candidates by being well prepared, forthright and energetic. That was all it took. She was not an electrifying public speaker, but she was highly competent and committed. She answered questions, and she was never afraid of answering back. She was admired for what was called her 'platform knowledge'. The future minister and newspaper editor Bill Deedes, who also first stood for Parliament at the 1950 election, remarked on the impact she made at meetings of prospective Tory candidates. 'Once she opened her mouth, the rest of us began to look rather second-rate,' he said, then added: 'Her knowledge and eloquence were a source of some irritation to her fellow candidates.' You feel this says as much about them as it does about her. Above all, she took herself and her ambitions seriously. That seems to have been enough to persuade others to let her pursue them.

||||
||||

It can be hard for any biographer to inject this faintly robotic tale with its share of drama. The challenge with the story of Margaret Thatcher's early years is to try to humanise it. Moore does his best by drawing on a previously unseen cache of letters from the young Margaret Roberts to her older sister, Muriel, written variously from Grantham, Oxford and Dartford. There she talks about boyfriends, fashion, shopping and the various inconveniences of life in wartime and then austerity Britain. These letters are, I suppose, human. But, boy, are they dull. The tone is hectoring, jolly and banal. Their most notable feature is the complete absence of any discussion of politics. Indeed, though the war and its aftermath made life bothersome in various ways, you would be hard pressed to guess from these letters that the young Margaret gave any thought to what it meant outside her domestic circle. She likes to dish out little Methodist homilies which seem incongruous rather than apposite given what was happening in the wider world. On the day Hitler invaded the Soviet Union in June 1941, she wrote à propos her own life experiences: 'A little thing is a little thing, but faithfulness in little things is a great thing.' In April 1945, she told Muriel about life at Oxford. 'The dons have dinner in their private dining-room during the vac, so there was no question of their company thank goodness. I had a marvellous dinner. First there was some lovely creamy soup and then some very tender lean beef [...] Finally there was some lemon jelly with lemon flavoured meringue on top.' There is no mention of the war. Perhaps she thought Muriel wouldn't be interested in her thoughts on politics. Perhaps her frame of reference is not so surprising in a young woman from the provinces. But given the person that young woman was to become, it is hard not to conclude that she had nothing to say because she had nothing to add. The war would continue on its course regardless of how thoroughly she boned up on it. Her suggestions for improvement, no matter how well informed, would not be heeded. So it didn't really exist for her. Her horizons expanded with her power to influence, not with her capacity to understand.

Another part of the Thatcher myth is that her early ambition went along with a clear set of principles that she stuck to through thick and thin. She was, on this account, nothing if not consistent. Moore quotes extensively from her youthful speeches and articles, suggesting that they laid out a basic philosophy of anti-collectivism and individual responsibility from which she never really deviated. This is not convincing. Mostly they read like boilerplate examples of sub-Churchillian rhetoric, scattered with snippets of romantic imperialism and paeans to the native resources of an island people. She believed in sound finance. So did almost everyone else at the time, including many members of the Labour Party. They just didn't know how to achieve it in a country that was more or less bankrupt. Nor did she. Before the 1950 election she told the voters of Dartford that the British spirit had to be rediscovered. 'Do you want it to perish for a soul-less Socialist system, or to live to re-create a glorious Britain? YOU WILL DECIDE.' Was any Tory candidate saying anything else? Insofar as there was substance to her early views, it was something from which she later diverged. During the 1950s she did not question the founding principles of Beveridge's welfare state. Her criticisms always focused on abuses of the system and how to prevent them, never on the need to reform the system itself. She accepted that even a proud island people required looking after by the state. It was not until much later that she began to think there might be an alternative.

More persuasive evidence of a consistent personal philosophy emerges only when she eventually entered Parliament. She lost both times in Dartford – it was not a winnable seat for the Tories until the 1970s – but she performed well and impressed everyone with her diligence. She then married Denis Thatcher, trained for the Bar (supported by his substantial wealth), had twins and, after a few painful rebuffs, found a safe seat for the 1959 election in Finchley. This produced one significant change of heart. The mild, unthinking anti-Semitism of her

early letters – she complained to Muriel of the '"tatty" tour-
ists: Jews and novo [*sic*] riche' she encountered in Madeira on
her honeymoon – gave way to a strong admiration for her
Jewish constituents, among whom she found many of the
values she herself cherished. 'My, they were good citizens,' she
later remarked, seeing Jews as 'natural traders' who managed
'positively to get on by their own efforts'. When she got to
Westminster, she benefited from another happy accident. She
came near the top of the lottery that gives individual back-
benchers the chance to propose new pieces of legislation. This
meant she could select a cause and use her maiden speech to
promote it. After some dithering she chose to introduce a bill
that would require local government to open itself up to more
regular reporting by the press; she wanted to prevent local officials from hiding their activities behind a veil of secrecy.

There has been some speculation about the psychological
motives for this choice. Her father, Alfred Roberts, had been
an alderman in Grantham and a leading figure in the town's
affairs until he was unceremoniously turfed out of office in
1952. Margaret admired him but also found him closed off and
unresponsive. Was this legislation a complex act of revenge
against his secretiveness (Roberts seems to have been, among
other things, a closet womaniser)? Or was it an act of revenge
against his enemies, designed to unmask the dirty tricks that
had seen her father deprived of his position? Probably it had
nothing to do with him. Thatcher believed that openness
would benefit the Tory cause, because when people saw how
their money was being spent they would become much more
careful about whom they entrusted it to. This was the thread
that connected her first legislative act with what became effectively her last: the poll tax. She wanted everyone to pay the
same for local government so that everyone would be forced to
think hard about whether they were getting value for money.
Of course, by that point her years in power had corroded her
judgement, allowing her to embark on a battle she lacked the

resources to win. Time ran out for her long before the poll tax could work its intended magic on profligate Labour councils. But her hope remained the same from first to last: Tories could win the argument so long as the requisite information was available for them to use and so long as they had the determination and energy to use it.

This made her an unusual Conservative. It also caused some of her opponents to misjudge her. Barbara Castle, who consistently both admired Thatcher and underestimated her, supported her Private Member's Bill in 1960 on the grounds that it could only aid the Labour Party in the long run. 'It is always the progressive movements which are supporters of publicity,' Castle said. 'It is conservatism which always needs secrecy to survive, and not socialism.' Thatcher thought the opposite. For someone like Castle this made her unfathomable: here was a Conservative who wanted to keep the argument going rather than close it down. It is a mistake that people on the left of politics often make: because they are so sure they are right and that the future belongs to them, they don't know what to do with opponents who believes time is on their side.

Thatcher was insatiable in her search for new ideas she could bring to the fight. She read heavyweight books – Adam Smith, Burke, Popper, Hayek – and carefully noted their contents. She enjoyed talking about these writers when she got the chance. But did she really understand them? One of the questions that has always dogged Thatcher is whether she was intellectually serious. There is plenty of contradictory evidence. Some people found her remarkably open to big ideas, always willing to debate questions of principle. Others found her blinkered and pedestrian, with an actuarial or lawyerly approach to political philosophy, ticking off useful concepts and ignoring the rest. The writer and journalist Paul Johnson (perhaps not the most reliable witness) described her as 'the most ignorant politician of her level that I'd come across until I met Tony Blair', but he thought she was at least touchingly aware of her ignorance, 'the eternal scholarship girl'. He summed it up by saying: 'I always liked her, but she always bored me a bit.' Being boring is a sin for an intellectual. But it is not always a sin in politics. The truth is that ideas were weapons for Thatcher, and she liked to use them in hand-to-hand combat. She was not, contrary to her reputation, a big-picture politician. She took the big pictures of others and fashioned them into sticks she could beat people with. The famous story of her banging a table with a copy of Hayek's *The Constitution of Liberty* – 'This, gentlemen, is what we believe!' – is revealing more for what she was doing than for what she was reading. Books were for making a point, forcefully enough for the point to carry.

IIII
IIII

When, in 1975, Thatcher stood for the leadership of the Conservative Party, she didn't present herself as an ideologue. Her pitch was that she was a politician willing to do what needed to be done. She had survived a near-death experience as education secretary in the Heath government, when her decision to scrap free milk in primary schools for children aged seven and over made her for a while the most unpopular politician in the country ('Milk Snatcher'). It had been a grisly time and had tested even her energy and resolve; people around her noticed how tired she became. The decision had been pressed on her by civil servants, and though she understood the cost-cutting benefits, she had not sufficiently thought through the political consequences. Typically, she resolved to be better briefed in future and to work harder; she also decided to spend more public money to reverse her reputation as a penny-pincher. She promised to expand nursery education, build more polytechnics and raise the school leaving age. It worked. Her reputation as a political pragmatist went up while that of the government she served went down, mired in its inability to control the unions. Heath as prime minister suffered from the double failing of being prickly but pusillanimous. (It subsequently emerged that these facets of his personality may have been exacerbated by an undisclosed thyroid condition that also had the unfortunate side-effect of making him fat; as he got plumper, Thatcher got thinner.) Heath wanted to micro-manage the economy but lacked the ability to exert his will. The new intake of Tory MPs who arrived following the twin elections of 1974, both of which Heath lost, had tired of what they saw as his arrogant assumption of expertise. One reported that the 'new MPs liked Margaret Thatcher and thought the rest of the front bench technocrats'. What she believed didn't matter as much as the fact that she wasn't put off by people refusing to accommodate their beliefs to hers. She was up for the fight. She didn't want to reach a lasting understanding with the unions. She wanted to avoid one.

She was hardly alone in this. By now parts of the Tory Party were festering with combative new thinking from people who had had enough of what they saw as Britain's managed decline. Thatcher was not the only standard-bearer for the anti-Heath factions. There was Edward du Cann, who represented swashbuckling capitalism, Keith Joseph, who represented high-minded anti-statism, and Geoffrey Howe, who repre-sented disciplined proto-monetarism. But she saw them all off easily. In this she was greatly helped by their obvious lack of leadership qualities. Du Cann was cavalier and untrustworthy; Joseph was flaky and depressive; Howe was deadly dull. She was also aided by the fact that she was a woman, married to a man like Denis. The other three were undone in part by their wives. Mrs du Cann and Mrs Joseph rightly suspected that their husbands were hopelessly unsuited to the demands of prime ministerial office and did what they could to dissuade them from standing. In the case of Elspeth Howe there were muttered suspicions that she would be the one wearing the trousers. The Conservative Parliamentary Party in its default gentlemen's club mode likes nothing more than chuntering on about the perils of a Lady Macbeth. (Elspeth Howe waited fifteen years to extract her revenge, helping her husband write the resignation speech that triggered Thatcher's demise.) The great advantage when Lady Macbeth takes the reins herself is that no one can suspect her of harbouring a Lady Macbeth in the background. Theresa May, supported by her unassuming husband, Philip, has also benefited from this inverted prejudice; it was her leadership rival Michael Gove who was suspected of being egged on by his unscrupulous journalist wife, Sarah Vine. After Thatcher told Denis that she planned to stand against Heath for the leadership, he did, in his own words, 'suck my teeth a bit. "Heath will murder you," I told her.' But once he realised she was determined, he gave her his unstinting support and was thrilled when she won.

The Thatcher marriage was not always plain sailing. As he was approaching fifty, five years after his wife had entered Parliament, Denis suffered a nervous breakdown, brought on by overwork (and no doubt overdrink), and went to South Africa for more than two months to recover. Neither party to the marriage could be entirely confident when he left that he would ever come back. But return he did, and when his wife was elected leader he retired from business to become her permanent consort and helpmeet. He almost certainly influenced her political views, on South Africa among other things, far more than Elspeth Howe ever did her husband's, or than Sarah Vine has Michael Gove's. Thatcher was never much good at reading a balance sheet, and she relied on Denis for advice. It was he who cast his eye over the books of British Leyland when she became prime minister and told her, against the advice of her civil servants, that the company was a basket case. But his main role was to prevent her from overdoing it, which was a perpetual hazard. He doesn't appear much in Moore's biography, but when he does it is often to curtail some late night session of booze-fuelled browbeating of her officials with the command: 'Bed, woman!'

||||
||||

The Tory leadership contest of 1975 looked like a fight between political pygmies compared with the Labour leadership contest that took place the following year. When Harold Wilson resigned as prime minister, the candidates lined up to replace him included Jim Callaghan, Roy Jenkins, Tony Benn, Anthony Crosland, Michael Foot and Denis Healey. It was, by any historical standards, an impressive cast list. The Parliamentary Labour Party made the right choice in plumping for Callaghan over the initial favourite, Healey, and the surprise early front-runner, Foot. Of all the political opponents Thatcher faced in her career Callaghan was by far the most formidable. He knew exactly how to deal with her. Because her preferred mode of attack was to hammer away, he gave her nothing to hammer at. He smothered her with what she called his 'avuncular flannel'. He patronised her. He teased her. Her Commons performances became increasingly frenetic and unconvincing as she ploughed on with her lists of complaints and he effortlessly batted them away. He also made sure that he was planted squarely on the centre ground of British politics, from which she struggled to dislodge him.

Thanks in part to the conditions imposed by the IMF after its bail-out of the British economy in 1976, Callaghan's government had embarked on a process of moderate reform, curtailing public spending and reaching relatively tough pay settlements with the unions. These measures steadied the ship, and by the summer of 1978 there were signs of economic recovery. Inflation had fallen to below 10 per cent from a peak of nearly 25 per cent three years earlier. Thatcher was being drawn more and more to hot-button social issues such as immigration in an attempt to extend her electoral appeal. She was in danger of losing the economic argument. But though Callaghan could deal with Thatcher, he couldn't deal with the endlessly frustrated hope, which he had inherited from Heath and Wilson, of achieving

a lasting settlement with the unions. He confounded expectations inside and outside his government by refusing to call an
election in the autumn of 1978. Instead, he chose to wait until a
new government directive establishing a 5 per cent norm for pay
increases could take effect. He was confident that by the following summer low inflation and a settled wage policy would be
enough to see off Thatcher, who could be painted as having no
alternative to offer except a free-market free-for-all. He would
stand for order. She would stand for chaos. He was wrong. As
Moore writes, Callaghan 'thought the 5 per cent rule would be
his salvation. In fact, it turned out to be his crucifixion.'

Over the next six months Callaghan lost control of his
political destiny and handed Thatcher hers. Instead of discip-
lining the unions, the 5 per cent rule emboldened them and
undermined the resolve of many employers, who decided
the policy was unsustainable. Ford Motors was one of the
first to break the terms of the agreement, and Callaghan,
who was trying to manage a minority government, lacked
the votes in Parliament to impose sanctions. On 12 December
the public sector unions rejected the government's pay deal,
which presaged a wave of strikes over the rest of the winter,
leaving rubbish to pile up in the streets and in some places
the dead to remain unburied. Thatcher was now the one in a
position to offer patronising and deliberately unhelpful advice.
She promised the government parliamentary co-operation if
it would ban secondary picketing, legislate for secret ballots
and work towards no-strike agreements with essential services
such as the Fire Brigade. She knew full well that Callaghan's
parliamentary weakness meant he was in no position to agree
these terms. His government limped on, struggling to patch
together wafer-thin majorities in the Commons until in April
it lost a motion of no confidence by a single vote. In the subsequent election campaign Callaghan outperformed Thatcher
on the stump, as he always did, but he knew it was too late. She
had come to stand for order. He stood for chaos.

But what sort of order? Thatcher arrived in office in May 1979 more clearly defined by what she wouldn't do than by what she would. She was the alternative to two approaches to politics that had both run out of road. One was consensus: at various points during the traumas of the 1970s it was mooted that only a national government of all the parties and all the talents could save the country (the octogenarian Harold Macmillan apparently spent much of the decade waiting for the call to lead such an administration from the House of Lords, which goes to show what an unrealistic idea it was). Thatcher's solid parliamentary majority of 43 put a stop to all such talk, at least for the time being. The other approach was confrontation: the Winter of Discontent had tested to destruction the idea that a managed wage policy could produce anything other than permanent antagonism between the government and the union movement, as each looked to see how far it could push the other.

Thatcher's alternative to both consensus and confrontation is conventionally understood to have been monetarism. A Thatcher government would withdraw from the industrial battlefield and focus its attention on tightening the money supply in order to attack the primary cause of inflation. Wage policy would be a matter for individual employers to determine, with the state's role limited to enforcing the rule of law (beefed up where necessary) in any confrontations that might ensue. The government would not seek industrial agreement, but neither would it attempt to impose its will by fiat. It would take a step back to create the monetary framework within which sustainable economic growth could be achieved without constant derailment by pressure-group politics and crisis management. The conventional understanding is, however, faulty. It is true that Thatcher was determined not to have a wage policy, and she stuck to that. It is also true that she had an initial go at monetarism. But she didn't stick to that. It turned out that her alternative to both confrontation and consensus was simply another sort of crisis management: she made it up as she went along.

Thatcher's personal attachment to monetarism was never very steady. She was no economist: as one of her advisers put it, she was 'good on finance [...] not good on economics'. She had read the high priest of monetarism, Milton Friedman (she and members of her shadow cabinet had met with him often), and she knew she wanted the same things he wanted: sound money, an end to stagflation, limits on government profligacy. But he was far from sure that she understood his prescription for getting there. There was one thing she liked even less than high inflation and that was high interest rates. They unnerved her because she felt she had direct experience of their effect on small businesses and ordinary families, especially those with mortgages. Her government's first foray into controlling the money supply included punitively high interest rates, which made her uncomfortable. They also made Friedman uncomfortable, because he thought this was the wrong way to tackle the problem: in his universe it was doing things back to front to use interest rates to control the money supply, rather than acknowledging that the rate of interest simply reflects the supply of and demand for money. Friedman wanted the Bank of England to print less of the stuff and let things take their course from there. But Thatcher did not have the time or the political patience to let things take their course. Her tough monetary stance had had the unintended side-effect of boosting the value of sterling, so making it much harder for British industry to export. Within a year of her coming to Downing Street, Thatcher's government was presiding over rapidly rising unemployment, stubbornly high inflation, an expanding money supply, sky-high interest rates and falling exports. It was time to try something else.

This is what she did in the autumn of 1980. Just as she was making her famous 'The lady's not for turning' speech to the party conference, the lady turned. She wanted lower interest rates. She also wanted a more competitive currency. Her government, under the direction of her chancellor, Geoffrey Howe, returned to traditional methods of exchange rate management through adjustments to interest rates and fiscal policy, hoping to patch together a short-term fix to get her over the worst. At the same time, she didn't want to signal any weakening of resolve. She turned her personal attention to getting the spending of government departments under control. This was much more her style. The trouble with Friedmanism was that it attacked the mechanics of money rather than the people who used it: that was its point, to depoliticise politics. The MPs who had decided in 1975 that Thatcher was no technocrat had been right. She had no desire to take the politics out of politics. She needed flesh-and-blood creatures to get after. So she went after her colleagues, subjecting them to the sort of harangues that drove some, such as Prior, to despair.

The economic situation was not improving. Unemployment was approaching levels that only months earlier had seemed politically suicidal. When the Tories launched their famous 'Labour Isn't Working' poster campaign in 1978, featuring a snaking queue for the dole office, the unemployment figure was just over one million. By June 1981 the figure was 2.6 million and it would pass 3 million at the start of 1982. Though she demanded resolve from others, she was perfectly capable of throwing in the towel herself when the occasion required it. In February 1981 she shied away from a fight with the miners, capitulating to NUM demands to abandon a plan of pit closures. The previous month, despite what Denis had told her about British Leyland being effectively bust, she signed off on a massive bail-out to prop up the business. By now some of her strongest supporters were starting to wonder whether her government had what it took. When the Leyland decision was announced by Keith Joseph, her closest ally in the cabinet and the secretary of state for industry, Alfred Sherman at the staunchly Thatcherite Centre for Policy Studies turned his framed photo of Joseph to the wall.

But even if the lady was for turning, she was not for giving up. The mistake made by the 'wets' in her government was to suppose that her intransigence had boxed her in. They thought she didn't understand the suffering and anger her policies were causing and, above all, that she was blind to the human cost of mass unemployment. They may have been right about this. But they were wrong to suppose that it followed that she would be unable to deal with the political consequences. The common failing of her opponents – within the Tory Party, on the Labour side and among the breakaway founders of the newly formed SDP – was their shared belief that she was a freakish aberration and that British politics would resume its regular course before long. They just had to wait their turn. This was a catastrophic error. A waiting game was what suited her best because it played to her strengths of resilience and remorselessness. Too many people at the top of British politics were biding their time in 1981, as riots broke out across the country and rising chaos looked ready to sweep her away. Too few were thinking about how they were going to stop her themselves. In public she announced that there was no alternative. But she had plenty of alternatives still to try. It was her opponents who appeared to lack them.

In 1981 she allowed Howe to persuade her of the need for an eye-wateringly tight budget, complete with tax rises, at a time when the conventional wisdom said only fiscal loosening could save her. It was tempting to suppose this must be the final nail in the coffin. Howe sold Thatcher on his budget by promising her lower interest rates in future, plus greater freedom of political manoeuvre once it was over. At the same time a group of 364 economists sent a letter to the *Times* condemning her economic policies (the signatories included

Mervyn King, the future governor of the Bank of England).
They wrote:

> There is no basis in economic theory or supporting
> evidence for the government's belief that by deflating
> demand they will bring inflation permanently under
> control and thereby introduce an automatic recovery in
> output and employment [...] The time has come to reject
> monetarist policies and consider which alternative offers
> the best hope of sustained recovery.

There were two things wrong with this letter. First, it mistook
Thatcher for an ideologue rather than a desperate politician
scrabbling around for options. Second, as Moore points out,
'it was significant that, beyond stating that alternative policies
existed, the *Times* letter did not say anything about them. As
with internal critiques by the wets, the letter was clear in its
revulsion at what the government was doing, but much less
confident about what to do instead.' The economists' intervention has since acquired legendary status as an example of
academic hubris and cack-handedness. 'The timing was exqui-
site,' Nigel Lawson wrote in his memoirs: almost from the day
the letter appeared, the leading economic indicators started to
pick up and the Thatcher boom was under way.

The recovery was hardly a ringing endorsement of monetarism. By reverting to the traditional give-it-a-go approach to
managing the economy, Thatcher had bought herself enough
breathing space to reap the benefits of a cyclical upturn, though
her policies ensured that it would be a long time before unemployment started to come down (the number of unemployed
began to fall only in the third quarter of 1986). By 1981 the
Labour Party was undergoing its own spasm of leftward revulsion under the leadership of Michael Foot. Thatcher knew that
so long as she lived to fight another day, she would get the
chance to fight Foot at the ballot box. She had to be in it if she

was going to win it. A group of MPs from the 1979 intake on the Tory back benches, who called themselves the Blue Chips and in October 1981 published a pamphlet called *Changing Gear*, were the only ones among her critics who got her remotely right. They included Chris Patten, John Patten, William Waldegrave and Tristan Garel-Jones, and were soon to be joined by John Major. In the pamphlet they used as an epigraph a line from Macmillan: 'We have at least the most important thing of all at the head of our government, a prime minister of courage, who I hope will not be led away from the old tradition of consensus.' The Blue Chips didn't attack the economic direction of the government, but they called for more political flexibility: 'A political strategy based on economic theory is a house built on sand.' Thatcher could agree with that, whatever she thought of their views on consensus. Her other critics she batted off. The Blue Chips she promoted over time into her government, and one of them, eventually, became her successor.

IIII

This wasn't the only area where Thatcher's brutally resilient adaptability was on display during her early years in power. In Northern Ireland she was confronted with IRA prisoners going on hunger strike in the Maze prison in an attempt to force the British government to recognise them as prisoners of war rather than regular inmates. The IRA leadership, which included Gerry Adams and Martin McGuinness, wanted a show of strength and was perfectly willing to see its men starve themselves to death to make its point. The more intransigent the British were the better, since the IRA was confident it had the greater appetite for the long game. In this the hard men may have been misled by Thatcher's gender: they assumed that she would find it hard to stomach young men dying on her watch, accompanied by the insistent grief of their families. But

Thatcher was flinty in public: she would not negotiate with terrorists. Behind the scenes, she was a little more accommodating. She told her cabinet colleagues: 'I am concerned to get us into the most reasonable position before the start, and stick to it.' She agreed to meet the IRA halfway on the question of prisoners' clothing (they could wear 'civilian-type' clothes). But even this overstated the firmness of her stance. Bobby Sands began his hunger strike on 1 March 1981, joined by a number of others. On 9 April, Sands was elected to the House of Commons in a by-election held in Fermanagh and South Tyrone. On 5 May he died. Thatcher came under immense international pressure, particularly from the United States and the Vatican, to do something. On 12 May a second hunger striker, Francis Hughes, died. The families of the other strikers started to worry that the British were going to let them all die. Brendan McFarlane, the IRA leader in the Maze, warned Gerry Adams: 'It appears they are not interested in simply undermining us, but completely annihilating us [...] They are insane – at least Maggie is anyway.' But Maggie too was exploring her options and looking for a way out.

Despite her public statements, her government was already involved in back-channel discussions with the IRA and the Irish government. She understood that the most important thing was not to get boxed in, so she allowed the Irish Commission for Justice and Peace, a Catholic body primarily concerned with aid to the Third World, to enter the Maze and to indicate that the British government was open to discussions on the hunger strikers' demands if they would stop their fast. Their IRA masters would not let them do that, but they did start talking about terms for ending the protest. The talks broke down, but they had the effect of raising expectations among the families of the remaining hunger strikers that their lives might be spared. This raised pressure on the IRA, and eventually it was their leaders who could not stomach the drip-drip-drip of the families' dashed hopes and futile grief.

To stoke this, the Thatcher government kept dangling its olive branch. By September 1981 ten prisoners had starved themselves to death. After beseeching pleas from their mothers, two hunger strikers gave up their fast. Horrible as it seems, it is hard not to read in this story a dry run of what was going to happen when Thatcher finally decided to take on the National Union of Mineworkers in 1984–5, which became the defining confrontation of her time in office. Public intransigence, private flexibility, the constant search for the weak spot that would undo the other side's resolve: the ruthlessness of a true political pragmatist.

The same qualities that meant Thatcher's reverses were never as bad as they appeared also meant her victories were never as complete as they were presented. She outlasted the hunger strikers, but she didn't achieve much by it except to ensure that the IRA would try to kill her if it got the chance (as it nearly did in the Brighton bombing of 1984). The great set-piece success of her first year in office – the European budget rebate she secured in May 1980 – was also something of a pyrrhic victory. She wanted far-reaching reform of European institutions, including the Common Agricultural Policy, which she rightly saw as a permanent barrier to change. But when she was offered a quick settlement and a chunk of cash, she took it. The newspapers hailed her as a warrior smiting the Eurocrats, but she and her officials knew she had merely put off the important battles. John Nott, her trade secretary, wrote her a memo which spelled it out: 'One of the misfortunes for me of the budget negotiations was that we had very nearly achieved this objective [CAP reform] […] but we lost the opportunity when we accepted a temporary settlement.' Thatcher's later bloody-mindedness over Europe was in part a result of her sense that she had blown her best chance.

However, it was much harder to gainsay the defining victory of her first term and the one that fixed her reputation for steely resolve around the world. On 2 April 1982 Argentinian forces invaded the Falkland Islands. A task force was quickly assembled to get them back, despite the many warnings Thatcher received that it would prove either politically or militarily impossible. It turned out to be neither. On 15 June Thatcher received a telegram confirming an Argentinian surrender that ended with the words: 'The Falkland Islands are once more under the government desired by their inhabitants. God save the Queen.' Thatcher knew that she probably could not have survived any other outcome, because it was her government's confused defence policy and diplomatic incompetence that had encouraged the Argentinians to try their hand in the first place. Once her foreign secretary, Lord Carrington, had resigned over these failings, she was next in the firing line. Her bloody-mindedness in this instance was fuelled by a sense of personal culpability: it was her mess to sort out. It took all her reserves of political graft to do it. There were many different aspects to the Falklands campaign, of which the most pressing wasn't always the military contest with Argentina's armed forces. Thatcher also had to deal with the Americans, who wanted a peaceful resolution to the conflict. This meant that for the first and only time in her career she was forced to square off against another woman, one almost as formidable as she was: Jeane Kirkpatrick, the US ambassador to the United Nations. Thatcher routed her as decisively as she did General Galtieri.

Kirkpatrick's importance derived not from her role at the UN but from her status as the author of the Kirkpatrick Doctrine, which helped to define the anti-Communist stance of the Reagan White House. In a paper of 1979 titled 'Dictatorships and Double Standards' she had argued that it was crucial to distinguish totalitarian regimes (always bad) from authoritarian ones (unpleasant but often amenable). In the fight against

Communism, the US had to be willing to work with authoritarians in order to hold the line against the Soviets and their allies, who were by Kirkpatrick's definition beyond the pale. The military junta in Argentina, which came to power in 1976 and was by the end of 1981 headed by Galtieri, became a test case for this approach. Galtieri may have been a thug. He may also have been a drunk. (When Reagan first phoned him to discuss the invasion of the Falklands, Galtieri was more or less incoherent from drink. My brother-in-law, who is Argentinian, was an eighteen-year-old conscript in 1982 and remembers having to tidy up one morning after Galtieri and his entourage had passed through; there were bottles piled up everywhere.) But at least Galtieri was not a socialist. Kirkpatrick thought that Thatcher did not properly understand the implications of what she was attempting: if the Falklands were retaken by force, the junta might fall, and then what? There had to be an amicable solution. Henry Kissinger too tried to get the point across. Lord Hailsham, who had picked up some house party gossip, relayed the message to Thatcher at cabinet: 'Kissinger said [...] that British were not aware of danger of Socialist Govt in Argentina.' What really mattered, however, was whether the message was getting through to Reagan. The entire British political establishment, Thatcher included, was neuralgically sensitive to the risks of another Suez, when lack of support in Washington had scuppered the whole enterprise. So it was essential that Reagan and his secretary of state, Alexander Haig, listen to Thatcher, not to Kirkpatrick.

To achieve this, Thatcher deliberately avoided getting sucked into geopolitical discussions with the president and his representatives. She stuck to a few basic points of principle – invasion of sovereign territory, outraged public opinion, our boys fighting and dying out there – then got down to details. She wore away at Reagan with her obsessive focus on logistics and the technical grounds for rejecting any proposed peace settlement. She was always much better informed than he was and able to dominate any discussion. Sometimes he barely got a word in. The UN secretary-general, Javier Pérez de Cuéllar, tried to get Reagan to bring Thatcher to heel. He did what he could, but it was never enough. Thatcher knew who was to blame: 'Mrs Kirkpatrick's behaviour had been very vexing and thoroughly anti-British.' Once British troops were fully engaged in the South Atlantic the prospects for any negotiated settlement receded, but Kirkpatrick carried on trying. She badgered Reagan to maintain the pressure for peace, and pleaded with Haig to authorise her to abstain on a ceasefire resolution that came to the UN Security Council on 4 June, rather than joining the British ambassador in vetoing it. Haig told her she had to support the British position for the sake of transatlantic solidarity, then at the last minute changed his mind and ordered an abstention. But the message arrived too late for Kirkpatrick, who had just cast a very reluctant veto. She then astonished everyone by announcing that 'if it were possible to change a vote once cast the US would like to change its vote from a veto to an abstention'. She followed this by reading out a poem by Borges about the horrors of war. Her humiliation was complete. So was Thatcher's triumph over her.

What this shows is that the common picture of Reagan and Thatcher as joined at the hip is thoroughly misleading. They were, in many ways, very different politicians. Reagan really did prefer the big picture, which is why Thatcher could so often get the better of him with her narrower focus and grinding attention to detail. He was broadly an optimist, whereas she was often fearful of the unexpected. He didn't share her preoccupation with interest rates, instead seeing inflation as always and everywhere the enemy. When Reagan arrived in the White House, eighteen months after Thatcher reached Downing Street, Thatcherism was being regularly derided in the US as a failed experiment, far too erratic and ill considered to arrest Britain's decline; it was, if anything, accelerating it. Reagan was expected to learn from her mistakes, not to follow her example. He was also being encouraged to see Britain as a minor and fading player in the broader transatlantic alliance. The continental Europeans were the people who really mattered.

They also mattered to Thatcher, who was much more willing to take Europe's side against the US than her reputation normally allows. She repeatedly warned Reagan against undermining the position of the social democratic West German leader Helmut Schmidt, whose political interests were not well served by the blanket anti-Communism coming out of Washington. It is easy to forget that Thatcherism in its initial phase was a broadly pro-German project. It took much of its inspiration from the West German economic miracle, achieved under the philosophy known as 'ordo-liberalism' (a free market in an ordered society). The German model was also sometimes referred to as the 'Social Market', and Keith Joseph had originally wanted to use this term for the title of what eventually became the Centre for Policy Studies (when a 'Social Market Foundation' was finally born in 1989, it served as a rump SDP think-tank before being colonised by New Labour). Thatcher had no problem at this stage with the Germans, and certainly no problem with the dashing Schmidt, whom she found personally very appealing. It is said that some of her officials at the time thought European gatherings could be expedited if she and Helmut simply got a room.

Thatcher's problems were all with the French. As leader of the opposition she had had a bad experience at a briefing with the director of the IMF, Pierre-Paul Schweitzer, 'a languid, cigarette-smoking French intellectual of the type she had probably never encountered before'. He condescended to her and treated her like an ignorant housewife. She also got on very badly with Giscard d'Estaing, another supercilious snob. Things improved when the French elected a socialist, François Mitterrand, as president. Mitterrand could relate to her personal vanity and knew how to appeal to it. The Falklands War helped. When Thatcher launched her task force, Mitterrand wondered: 'Do I admire her or envy her?' When it was over, she returned the compliment: 'He was most understanding and splendid throughout.'

In the aftermath of the Falklands it became clear just how haphazard and contingent her political friendships and alliances were. If you stuck up for her when the chips were down, you were in ('one of us'); if you didn't, you were out. Those she felt had been 'staunch' in the war included – alongside Mitterrand – Pinochet, King Hussein of Jordan and David Owen of the SDP. (Owen seems to have been one of the surprisingly large number of men who found Thatcher intensely sexually desirable. Moore reports him telling the TV interviewer Brian Walden, off the record: 'The whiff of that perfume, the sweet smell of whisky. By God, Brian, she's appealing beyond belief.') The Falklands may have helped convert Thatcher to the cause of environmentalism. She remained deeply attached to the work of the British Antarctic Survey, whose maps had shown the terrain of the islands before the task force landed. Not only did she make sure they received a disproportionate amount of government funding thereafter, but she also listened to them when they warned of the damage being done to the ozone layer by pollution. One of the things that has often puzzled people about Thatcher is that she later became almost the first major politician to take the threat of climate change seriously. The role of the British Antarctic Survey in the preparations for the Falklands War helps explain why: it was more or less random, like many of her alliances.

Thatcher's focused, blinkered, relentless style of politics didn't bring clarity, as is so often claimed. It brought a hotchpotch of small revolutions that could appear like, but didn't amount to, a much larger one. Along with her fixations she had massive blind spots. One was Scotland, a part of the United Kingdom she never really understood or cared seriously about. Her neglect (or worse) helped to create the conditions for the rise of the SNP and the destruction of Tory support in Scotland. Thatcher was also thoroughly neglectful of the scope for her economic reforms to unbalance the British economy. She never thought through the possibility that her right-to-buy scheme for council homes would create a housing shortage in the long run and fuel a destructive property bubble. The present mess in British politics – from Brexit to the strains of devolution to the financial crisis and its aftermath – owes as much to the incoherence of her political thinking as it does to her supposed radicalism.

Yet most of the leading British politicians who have followed her have wanted in some way to be her. This includes, of course, Theresa May, who still burns at the thought that Thatcher beat her to the title of Britain's first woman prime minister. But it also includes Tony Blair, who saw in Thatcher the kind of game-changing politician he aspired and failed to be, and Cameron, who admired Thatcher's ability to turn ideology into practical political results, something he too failed to achieve. 'We are all Thatcherites now,' Cameron said by way of tribute after her death. Even Jeremy Corbyn, whose political convictions were shaped in the Thatcher years by his determination to represent all that she opposed, still exists to some extent in her shadow.

Corbyn was personally associated during the mid- to late 1980s with the three organisations that Thatcher came to regard as 'the enemy within': the National Union of Mineworkers, led by Arthur Scargill, the Greater London Council, led by Ken Livingstone, and the IRA, represented by the Sinn Féin leaders Martin McGuinness and Gerry Adams. Corbyn was friends with them all. Thatcher abolished the GLC, broke the NUM and survived the IRA. Somehow Corbyn has long outlasted all those battles and reached the remarkable position of leading the Labour Party thirty years after the period that defined him as a politician. The hope Thatcher represents for Corbyn is that a leader who comes seemingly from nowhere, and who lacks many of the qualities expected of a prime minister, could yet turn out to be the defining politician of the age. Thatcher surfed the social and economic changes of the 1970s so that she was in a position to ride the wave of the 1980s. Corbyn would like to do the same for the 2010s on into the 2020s. Thatcher showed what can be done by a prime minister who is in the right place at the right time. But she also shows the importance of having the right personality to exploit that good fortune. Without it, chance would not be enough. Yet with it, chance often ends up setting the agenda.

Thatcher was a remarkable politician. But she left a terrible mess in her wake, and it's unclear why anyone would want to emulate her in that. 'She hated muddle, but she also caused it,' John Ashworth, her first chief scientist, said. It could serve as her epitaph.

3

BILL CLINTON

IN 1999, THE PENULTIMATE YEAR of the Clinton administration, George Stephanopoulos published a breathless memoir of his time in the White House entitled *All Too Human: A Political Education*. Stephanopoulos had been the president's press secretary and a close aide, so this was an insider's account. The book chimed with the *Zeitgeist*: its appearance coincided with Clinton's Senate trial, following his impeachment, and also with the first appearance on US television of *The West Wing*, which offered the fantasy of a different kind of liberal president. Stephanopoulos made working in Clinton's West Wing sound thrilling, monstrous, deranged. A group of super-smart men – and one or two women – fought round the clock to pin down their super-smart, hopelessly promiscuous president (promiscuous with his time, his interests, his attention, as well as in the more obvious ways). Speeches got written at the last moment, policy was endlessly being reformulated, old enemies were reached out to, while a train of new enemies was picked up along the way.

Stephanopoulos describes how important physical proximity to the president was – having your office a few yards nearer to the Oval Office than the next person was crucial – and he lets his readers know that he got close. This was more like a medieval court than a modern workplace, both deeply hierarchical and frighteningly chaotic. And there at the heart of it was George, fixing, fighting, cajoling, despairing, scheming, outwitting, getting outwitted and all the time feeding off the power. At one point our hero (George, not Bill) takes a fancy to Jennifer Grey, Patrick Swayze's co-star in *Dirty Dancing*, and he gets his people to sound out her people about whether she fancies a date. Yes she does! Stephanopoulos goes to gatherings of Greek-Americans, and they crowd round wanting to know when he is going to lift the curse of Dukakis (which says that short Greek men can't get elected president, because they look ridiculous in tanks). What can George do but shrug and smile – who knows?

Well, it turns out that the US was due an African-American president long before it was due a Greek-American one, something that would have seemed pretty incredible in 1999. Stephanopoulos became a breakfast TV host, occasional journalist and, like everyone else, first a blogger and then a tweeter. Nevertheless, it comes as a shock reading *The Clinton Tapes*, Bill Clinton's real-time reflections of his time in the White House, to discover just how little George mattered to Bill during the time when Bill meant so much to George. Stephanopoulos hardly features at all in the write-ups of a series of nearly eighty taped conversations that Taylor Branch had with Clinton over the course of his presidency. On the few occasions he does get noticed it is as a minor irritant and something of a buffoon. He gets only one sustained mention, in early 1996, when Bill and Hillary are griping about the torrent of scurrilous journalism that surrounds his presidency and their marriage:

> There was no end to it [… they] cited a *New Yorker* essay full of barbed quotes about Hillary from [Sally] Quinn and Elizabeth Dole, the senator's wife, plus a popular new novel about the 1992 election, *Primary Colors*. All she knew of that book, said Hillary, was that she cussed like a sailor and was portrayed in a graphic one-night

stand with George Stephanopoulos, of all people. Her
aggrieved mood dissolved into mirth.

At least Hillary cares enough to laugh at the thought of getting
into bed with Stephanopoulos. Bill hardly seems bothered.

Working for a president can be a frustratingly one-way
relationship. People who obsess about their boss often find that
their boss barely notices them. Even by those standards Clinton
seems to have been deeply unconcerned by the comings and
goings of his political staff. *The Clinton Tapes* gives a view of
the presidency as seen from the private quarters (where most
of the recordings took place) rather than the West Wing, and it
turns out that as seen from the private quarters the West Wing
barely registers. Of course, that may have been the point of
these conversations, which Clinton set up with his old friend
Branch (they had been room-mates together while working
on George McGovern's disastrous presidential campaign of
1972) in order to record for posterity a personal overview of
his presidency removed from the hurly-burly of his day-to-
day activities. Branch is constantly prodding him to reflect on
the weightier challenges that face him, particularly in foreign
affairs. Nevertheless, there is enough straying from these
topics, as Clinton unburdens himself, often late at night, to
give a strong sense of his real preoccupations. This is a unique
picture of what it feels like to be president as a presidency is
unfolding – or, at least, what it felt like to be Bill Clinton.

That said, we aren't provided with verbatim transcripts
of the president's words – Clinton still has those for release
one day to his presidential library in Arkansas – but instead
a curious, twice-removed version of the conversations, with
Branch having to reconstruct what was said from the notes he
made at the time. Yet the account he provides is sufficiently
artless – full of digressions, long-windedness, false starts and
nagging obsessions – to have the ring of authenticity. We get
interminable riffs about Clinton's golf game, which Branch

manages to convey were as dull to him as they were gripping for the president. At moments Clinton rants and rages, at others he becomes tearful, occasionally he gets bored, and sometimes he even falls asleep. One memorable exchange, just after he has been trounced in the 1994 midterm elections, begins with Clinton in the White House barber's chair, exhausted and frequently nodding off mid-sentence, only to rouse himself for a renewed bout of defiance and self-pity before slumping back again. Branch leaves him still talking to himself, and wonders if the president is suffering from narcolepsy, or something worse.

Through all this a clear picture of Clinton's passions and priorities emerges. The things he loves are politics, hard data and his family, in roughly that order. The thing he hates is the media: above all, newspapers, on which he blames almost all his troubles. His love of politics is not a love of the sort of low-level politicking in which Stephanopoulos and his fellow staffers indulge. Rather, he has an unquenchable fondness for politicians themselves, with all their foibles and all their weaknesses – it is, in other words, a kind of self-love. One of the recurring themes of the book, on which Branch frequently remarks, is Clinton's indulgent affection for many of his Republican opponents, notwithstanding the fact they spent most of his tenure in the White House trying to destroy him by fair means or foul, mainly foul. 'Good ol' Jesse' is all Clinton will say of the poisonous, racist Jesse Helms, who has just called him 'unfit' to lead the armed forces and warned him to stay away from North Carolina for his own safety. The newspaper obsession with Whitewater drives him mad, but not the Republican desire to capitalise on it, which he entirely understands. This is from 1997:

> After a White House parley, he had asked Senator Alan Simpson in confidence whether Republican strategists really believed the Clintons did something terrible in Whitewater, like theft or perjury. He mimicked the

hearty response. 'Oh, hell no,' cried Simpson. 'But our goal is to make people *think* you did, so we can pay you Democrats back for Iran-Contra.' Clinton chuckled with appreciation. Politicians understood payback.

He dishes out the same kid-glove treatment to Bob Dole, Newt Gingrich, even John Major, whom he was meant to despise because of the help the Tories had offered to Republicans trawling for smears during the 1992 election. 'I kind of like old John,' Clinton says at one point, 'but a lot of people don't.' In fact, Clinton has more kind words to say about Major than he does about Tony Blair, who was perhaps too much of an easy catch for Clinton's tastes, as well as being a bit squeaky clean. Clinton liked politicians who played dirty, because they made him feel better about his own peccadilloes. He also liked anyone who was susceptible to his charms, which was true of many more politicians than it was of newspaper journalists. Most of all, though, what Clinton liked about his Republican opponents was that he was better at politics than they were.

||||

Part of this was luck. Clinton was fortunate in the Republican challengers he faced: George Bush senior, Gingrich and Dole were all hopelessly inadequate to the task of outmanoeuvring such a skilful politician, especially when economic conditions were working in his favour, as they were for Clinton throughout his presidency. There is no denying the skill, however. Gingrich came closest to proving a worthy opponent, following his triumph in the 1994 midterms, but then he horribly overplayed his hand, allowing Clinton to call his bluff during the government shutdown of 1995. One of the pleasures of witnessing this presidency from the inside is watching Clinton first grasp, then husband, then exploit and finally drive home the fact that Gingrich had blown it. Clinton was invariably one if not two steps ahead of his rivals, always better informed, always more curious than they were about what might be coming next. At one point in the early stages of the 1996 campaign Branch asks him 'whether he focused on the grand strategies or the daily polls and individual states. "All of those," he replied. "I think about all of those."'

His appetite for information was insatiable, whatever the subject. When he talks to Branch about technical problems at the Hubble telescope, he knows all the names and functions of the various parts that have gone wrong. In 1997 Bill and Hillary plan a celebration for their daughter Chelsea's seventeenth birthday, but Hillary is late, so, Branch recounts, 'Clinton found himself the delighted sole host to a dozen high school girls in raucous discussions of love and the world.' Given his track record with young women in the White House, it's easy to imagine the worst. But a few pages later we discover what really turned Bill on about the occasion: he used it as an opportunity to give them all a little lecture about the scientific and moral implications of the cloning of Dolly the sheep. This desire to acquire new knowledge and then deploy it never disappears. Branch meets with him in 2001, after he has left the White House, and Clinton expresses some relief at being free from its burdens, but also some regrets. 'He had been studying these massive power outages in California. They were very complex, but it was basically a case of deregulation wretchedly done. "I could fix that," he said, slipping into talk of interlocking grids and overtaxed spot markets.' It is just about possible to imagine another politician talking like this, but surely no one else could have sounded wistful about it. There are moments when his inability to waste any piece of information makes Clinton seem a little mad. After Major's defeat by Blair in the 1997 election, Clinton tells Branch that he still has a soft spot for him, 'despite their political differences, and remarked oddly that Major seemed to slump forward because the back of his head was square rather than round'. It's as though he can't resist finding his own explanation for everything. The conversation moves swiftly on to a discussion of Iranian clerical politics, about which, unsurprisingly, Clinton is very well informed.

Yet despite these occasional glimpses of weirdness, what is really distinctive about Clinton is the way he brought together political gifts that do not often sit easily with each other. He was a unique combination of analytical dispassion and empathetic compassion. He could switch effortlessly from number-crunching to deep listening mode and back again. Above all, what he wanted to know was what makes you tick, whoever you were and wherever you came from. During one memorable visit to the White House, Boris Yeltsin ended up in his underpants on Pennsylvania Avenue trying to hail a cab to find him a pizza. Why, Clinton wants to know, does this man drink so much? He contemplates calling Mrs Yeltsin in for a heart-to-heart, and maybe even staging an intervention. You get the feeling there is nothing he would enjoy more than trawling through Yeltsin's childhood, looking for clues and spinning yarns about the drunks he knew back in Arkansas, including his own stepfather. Among world leaders, only Jiang Zemin remained entirely immune to his charm, and this nags away at Clinton far more than the intractable business of US–Chinese trade relations.

On the whole, Clinton emerges as a consistently shrewd judge of political character, but he invariably needs some biographical detail to make a connection. He gets it badly wrong in 1995, when he spends most of the year worrying obsessively about Colin Powell, whom he suspects of planning to run for the presidency and fears is the one person who could beat him. When Powell decides not to run, these anxieties suddenly look silly, but Clinton can't let it drop. 'The mistaken prediction about Powell seemed to gnaw at Clinton,' Branch writes. 'His mental churn pulled up a fresh clue. Every upward step for Powell had been paved by patronage and appointment, observed Clinton, including his post in the Reagan White House. Powell was a career staff officer at heart.' In the end Clinton nailed his man, as Powell's ineffectual spell as George W. Bush's secretary of state was to show.

Something else Clinton gets right in the end is the 2000 presidential election, where we see him becoming increasingly fretful about Al Gore's ability to beat Bush. Among domestic politicians Bush stands out as being entirely immune to Clinton's charms – a striking point of overlap with China's autocrats – and Clinton comes away from a private dinner in early 1999 having found him 'miserable and hostile the whole time'. As a reformed drunk, Bush was nothing like Yeltsin: he had already arrived at his moment of truth and needed no help from Clinton. But though Clinton reciprocates Bush's dislike for him, he does not share his disdain. As always, he admires Bush's brutal political instincts and his willingness to do whatever it takes to fight the election on his own ground. Clinton sees Bush as having reduced the campaign to three basic elements – personality, prosperity and partisanship – on the assumption that if he can win on two of these three fronts he will win the White House. Recounting a conversation in August 2000, three months before the election, Branch describes Clinton as 'rattled'. 'Bush's strategy denigrated the politics Clinton loved. At the same time, Bush aimed to win votes by doing so, which was politics, and therefore he earned Clinton's grudging admiration.' What Clinton feared was that Gore was playing into Bush's hands by trying to distance himself from the tawdriness that surrounded the Clinton White House post-Lewinsky. Gore had to run on the record, Clinton felt, because he would lose on personality. Prosperity should have been Gore's winning card, but by appearing to hold his nose at what had gone on under Clinton he made it too easy for Bush to associate the Clinton years with scandal instead.

Of course, Gore didn't agree, and even at third hand (via Clinton via Branch) one senses his exasperation at the idea that

Clinton had the answers when, as he saw it, Clinton himself was the problem. These deep tensions only finally came to a head at a meeting Clinton had with Gore after the election was lost. The idea was for each man to say what he thought had gone wrong, in a spirit of reconciliation, but they are soon baring their teeth. Gore can't get past Lewinsky, and Clinton can't get past the fact that Gore is still using Lewinsky as an excuse for all the failings of his campaign, including his inability to generate a coherent message. Gore wants Clinton to apologise to him personally for what he did, whereas Clinton feels he has been doing nothing but apologising. As Clinton saw it, 'Gore was merely revealing himself a creature of Washington and the press, soaked in spin-cycle indignation that Clinton could never apologise earnestly or completely enough.' Here is the ultimate insult in the Clinton lexicon: Gore had been posturing like a journalist when he should have been thinking like a politician. For Gore, Clinton is the posturer because he can never come clean about the demons that drive him. This gives Gore the moral high ground. But Clinton has the killer political argument. 'By God,' Branch has him exclaim, 'Hillary [who was winning her New York Senate seat at the same time Gore was losing the presidency] had a helluva lot more reason to resent [me] than Gore did, and yet she ran unabashedly on the Clinton-Gore record. With that clarity, she came from 30 points down to win by double digits.'

Who can say whether one person really loves another? But on this account, at least, Bill appears to be genuinely fond of his wife, and genuinely frightened of her. He is thrilled when she becomes a senator, and he shows plenty of respect for her political judgement – she spots that Colin Powell is all medals and no trousers well before he does. Yet behind this solicitousness it's not hard to see the guilt bubbling away, as it does in Clinton's relationship with Chelsea, whom he adores, pampers and, of course, betrays, as he betrays everyone in the end. In one extraordinary scene Clinton wrestles with the question of

whether he can go to Japan on important state business at a
time when Chelsea is about to take some exams. 'Clearly dis-
traught,' Branch writes, 'he sifted implications like a medieval
scholastic. It was a choice between public duty on a vast scale
and the most personal devotion, with potential hurt feelings on
all sides.' To get this in perspective: the exams are junior-year
midterms; the Japanese trip is to apologise for the deep offence
Clinton has caused by sending Gore in his place to an earlier
economic summit attended by other heads of government.
What is going on? When Gore discovers that the president is
struggling with this dilemma, he concludes, understandably,
that Clinton has lost his mind. Branch is generally restrained
in using hindsight to explain what might lie behind his conversations with Clinton. But he can't resist letting us know that
this particular exchange took place during the government
shutdown of late 1995, 'which had just facilitated his first two
groping assignations with young Monica Lewinsky'.

||||
||||

Clinton can do dispassion. He can do compassion. What he
doesn't do is contrition. Not then. Not now. Twenty years of
watching both Clintons refuse to apologise for those assignations with Lewinsky and the way the two of them behaved
in their aftermath has taught us that. Notwithstanding his
vast appetite for new knowledge, self-knowledge is not what
Clinton was after. He doesn't do introspection either: his obsessive, almost prurient interest in other people is partly there to
prevent him having to think too hard about himself. On the
rare occasions Branch gets him to reflect on what might lie
behind his personal failings the results are fairly excruciating. During a conversation in August 1999, after Clinton has
been provoked by a reporter's question about what Hillary
might have meant by 'her insinuation that he was emotionally
scarred', Branch says that 'something welled up':

'I think I just cracked,' he said, over and over. He felt
sorry for himself. When this thing started with Lewinsky
in 1995, he had gone through a bad run of people dying
at the start – his mother, Vince Foster [his old friend from
Arkansas who committed suicide after being brought
to Washington as a White House counsel, prompting
a wave of conspiracy theories], Rabin – plus the mean-
spirited investigations of him and Hillary and everybody
else [...] He had just cracked. He said he could have done
worse. He could have blown something up.

Well, he did blow something up – a pharmaceuticals factory
in Sudan, three days after he had been forced to confess to
the affair on national television in the summer of 1998. As for
dragging the death of Yitzhak Rabin into it, Yigal Amir, Rabin's
assassin, can be blamed for a great deal, but not for the fact that
Clinton wound up, in Branch's deathless description, placing
'his unlit cigar playfully in [Lewinsky's] vagina'.

If Clinton was haunted by Rabin's death, it was for political, not psychosexual, reasons. No one knows whether Rabin
would finally have been able to conclude a peace deal with
the Palestinians, but Clinton, along with many others, became
persuaded that his assassination had made it more or less
impossible. Clinton's failure to broker a peace in the Middle
East remained to his mind the greatest missed opportunity of
his presidency. Even if he doesn't do contrition, he certainly
does regret. In particular, he seems tortured by having come
so close but been unable to find the missing piece of the jigsaw.
It was not an isolated failure, however. Clinton did nothing to
prevent the genocide in Rwanda, and he made little headway
in stopping the carnage in Bosnia, where he seems not to have
known what to do, or how to deal with Milošević, until Tony
Blair's enthusiasm for war persuaded him to bomb the Serbs
out of Kosovo in 1999. Someone who got to know Clinton
well once told me that although he was one of the smartest

people he had ever met, he was fundamentally non-strategic. One or two steps ahead was his forte, not three or four, never mind five or six. Clinton liked to know, and was brilliant at foreseeing, what might come next. But he would get frustrated if he had to go beyond that, given how many other interesting things there were out there.

His mixture of charm and short-term attention to detail wasn't enough to make the difference in international politics: overseas politicians would be charmed by him but then ignore him, and no amount of number-crunching could change the fact that other countries' elections weren't his to fight. We see him in May 1996, 'talking intently on the phone about poll data in Israel'. But he is powerless to do anything about what he hears:

> District by district, he kept asking if that was all, writing down the numbers. Apparently Shimon Peres had done well in the only debate scheduled with his challenger, Benjamin Netanyahu [...] He had gained one point overall in the post-debate polls, building his nationwide lead to 3 per cent. The president looked resigned when he hung up. Three points were not enough, he said. Israeli elections always closed in the last few days towards the war party.

As usual, the president was right. To which eventual winner, Netanyahu, would have said: so what?

The one place outside the United States that did suit Clinton's brand of politics was Northern Ireland. Clinton describes each of his trips there with something like rapture. When the people of Northern Ireland vote in favour of the Good Friday agreement in May 1998, Clinton is euphoric, and in his element. 'He analysed majorities of 51–54 per cent by district,' Branch tells us, and he 'beamed'. But Clinton is shrewd enough to know that Northern Ireland is not like the Middle

East. Reflecting on the difference between his successes and his failures in a conversation recorded just twelve days before the end of his presidency, he gives Branch his final verdict:

> Peace-making quests came in two kinds: scabs and abscesses. A scab is a sore with a protective crust, which may heal with time and simple care. In fact, if you bother it too much, you can reopen the wound and cause infection. An abscess, on the other hand, inevitably gets worse without painful but cleansing intervention. 'The Middle East is an abscess,' he concluded. 'Northern Ireland is a scab.'

Yet because Clinton doesn't do introspection, he doesn't go on to draw the obvious inference: he was a scab president. The US during the Clinton years was booming, for reasons that had a little to do with his presidency (welfare reform, a balanced budget) and a lot to do with factors beyond his control (the end of the Cold War, improved telecommunications, the Fed's permanent propitiation of Wall Street, the growth of the housing and internet bubbles). The politics of this period was lurid and ugly on the surface, but underneath everything seemed fine. During and after the Lewinsky scandal Clinton drew great comfort from the fact that his approval ratings rarely dipped below 60 per cent and were higher at the end of his presidency than they had been at the beginning. But he doesn't stop to ask if this was because people liked him and his policies, and forgave him his indiscretions, or because they were too busy making money and watching television to care much either way.

The trouble with a scab presidency is that it doesn't leave much of an impression behind: it's not only the ugliness that is superficial. One of the striking features of George W. Bush's time in office was how quickly, and easily, he was able to dispense with Clinton's legacy and start doing things his way,

notwithstanding a practically non-existent mandate from
the voters. Of course, the American political system gives all
new presidents a relatively free hand, and makes it hard for
any administration to exercise much hold on the next. Still,
Clinton had hoped for much more. He believed, for instance,
that his relentless efforts to balance the budget would educate
the American people into understanding the importance of
long-term planning and fiscal responsibility. Then Bush came
along and scrapped all that, plunging straight into tax cuts and
deep deficits, and the American people simply shrugged and
pocketed what was offered to them. Clinton complained to
Branch in one of their final interviews that 'Bush was uncomfortable with foraging, creative, institutional leadership. He
wanted to point out the bad guys and lead a charge.' Clinton
himself was certainly foraging, and in his own way he was creative, but his reforms did not have deep institutional roots. He
was too catholic in his interests and his tastes, constantly on
the look-out for new challenges and diversions, always keen to
demonstrate what he might be able to add to any topic. In the
end, it was too much about him. He left the White House with
the American people sated but distracted and the Democratic
Party drained and demoralised. It's hard not to finish reading
about his presidency feeling the same way.

Clinton's final frustration was that he was denied by the
constitution from running for a third term, so that it could
have carried on being all about him. He was sure, and he was
surely correct, that he could have defeated Bush in 2000. There
has been a lot of speculation about what might have happened
on 9/11 if it had been Gore in the White House instead of
George W. Bush, but it is just as interesting (albeit just as idle)
to think about what might have followed had Clinton still been
there. Would he have seen the confrontation with Islamic terrorism as a 'scab' problem, to be carefully watched and given
time to heal, or an 'abscess', which required some deep inci-
sions? Would he have been blamed for what happened, as the

public woke up to the institutional deficiencies of his scatter-gun approach, or would he have steered the nation round to a mature and seasoned response, as he effortlessly managed following the Oklahoma City bombing in 1995? As it is, we know what did happen: Bush and the people behind him were already itching for some bloodletting, and the knives were drawn long before the smoke had cleared. This left the US with two gaping wounds – haemorrhaging public finances and an unwinnable war in Afghanistan – that Barack Obama, Clinton's ultimate heir, was unable to heal. During his wife's epic struggle with Obama in 2008, Clinton occasionally let his frustration boil over, no doubt feeling that he could have beaten Obama, and then trounced McCain, had he been running himself. But by that point it really wasn't about him any more. As the Obama presidency turned into the Trump presidency, and Clinton had to watch his wife lose once again to a candidate both Clintons believed was far beneath her, American politics has come to seem more and more like an abscess. All Clinton left it with were sticking plasters.

4

TONY BLAIR

TONY BLAIR EMERGES from his memoirs a man of extraordinary intellectual self-confidence. As prime minister, he liked to think for himself, and decide for himself, whatever the issue. He takes this to be one of the key attributes of leadership, and it is why he believes he was cut out for it while other people – above all, his chief rival, Gordon Brown – were not. But he also puts it down to his training as a barrister at the hands of the celebrated Derry Irvine, someone he describes as having 'a brain the size of a melon'. From Irvine, Blair learned the importance of what he calls 'drilling down' when faced with a seemingly intractable problem. What this means is being willing to go back to first principles, 'behind and beneath the conventional' analysis, and if necessary to look at the problem from a completely new angle. Time and again, when faced with a political difficulty, Blair describes taking himself away from his advisers and cabinet colleagues in order to sit and think on his own. But he does not limit himself to contemporary politics. He also likes to dig down into the past, looking for the solutions that escaped some of his predecessors. He thinks he knows better, and not just with the benefit of hindsight.

The most arresting example of this comes when Blair finds himself at Chequers one day 'meandering through the bookcases', as he puts it, and pulls down a volume of Neville

Chamberlain's diaries, which includes an account of his meeting with Hitler at Berchtesgaden prior to the Munich conference in 1938. Blair is struck by how unfairly history has treated Chamberlain. 'We are taught that Chamberlain was a dupe; a fool, taken in by Hitler's charm. He wasn't. He was entirely alive to his badness.' Chamberlain knew, according to Blair, that he was dealing with a madman. So why did he try to appease him? How could he get it so right, but get it so wrong? Blair's answer is that Chamberlain did not ask himself the right question. 'Chamberlain was a good man, driven by good motives. So what was the error? The mistake was in not recognising the fundamental question. And here is the difficulty of leadership: first you have to be able to identify that fundamental question.' Chamberlain thought that the question was: can Hitler be contained? In many ways, Blair concedes, this was the obvious thing to ask.

> Chamberlain should have been right. Hitler had annexed Austria and Czechoslovakia. He was supreme in Germany. Why not be satisfied? How crazy to step over the line and make war inevitable.
>
> But that wasn't the fundamental question. The fundamental question was: does Fascism represent a force that is so strong and rooted that it has to be uprooted and destroyed? Put like that, the confrontation was indeed inevitable. The only consequential question was when and how.

Chamberlain's problem was that he didn't drill deep enough.

This story inevitably brings to mind Blair's own wars. Yet in his autobiographical account of his time in office the discussion of appeasement comes not, as you might expect, in the more than one hundred pages Blair devotes to Iraq but in a section on public service reform and the Labour Party's reluctance to press ahead with it during his first term at the pace he would like. It provokes Blair to wonder if he has been asking the right question. 'Maybe the real problem wasn't the party's failure to embrace modernisation [...] Maybe it was that the country didn't really buy it. What if instead of taking on the party, I had to take on the public, my allies, the strong trunk holding up my branch?' It is hard to know what to make of this, or how a Hitler analogy could possibly help him resolve the dilemma. But it is also hard to avoid the thought that Blair is himself shirking the real question. He faced two serious and determined enemies during his time in Downing Street: Al-Qaeda and Gordon Brown. One, he concluded, represented a force so strong and rooted that it had to be uprooted and destroyed, since confrontation was inevitable; the only question was when and how. The other had to be contained, because stepping over the line would have been crazy and made war inevitable. But why on earth did he think that Al-Qaeda was an example of the first, and Gordon Brown an example of the second, rather than the other way round?

Blair did not have to appease Gordon Brown. He could have sacked him, particularly once he had accepted, as he did early on in his second term, that Brown was determined to obstruct him and ultimately to drive him out of Downing Street. Why didn't he do it? Blair asks himself this question more than once, and each time he is driven to the same conclusion: that having Brown 'inside and constrained was better than outside and let loose, or, worse, becoming the figurehead of a far more damaging force well to the left'. Blair takes these reflections to be more evidence of his ability to see things other people miss, and whenever some of his closest advisers try to persuade him he is wrong, and that his relationship with Brown is actually crippling the government, he reminds them that 'these judgments are the reason why I am leader and you are not!' Yet it is striking how timid and conventional Blair's analysis really is. Blair was – until Iraq – a prime minister in a position of almost unparalleled strength: massive majorities, quiescent opposition, remarkably steady economic growth. It is true that Brown claimed the credit for the last, but the easiest way to test that would have been to remove him and see if the economy kept growing. Sacking Brown would have been messy, unpleasant and unpredictable. It might have led to open warfare inside the party. But Blair does not explain to us why he believed it was a war he could not win. He insists he was not intellectually intimidated by Brown – Gordon might have had 'the better degree', but Tony considered himself far superior in political imagination and creativity. Blair would have us believe that he was a smarter politician, a deeper thinker and a better man than his rival. Yet still he did not dare touch him. Why not?

The answer is that digging down was Blair's weakness, not his strength. He was always on the look-out for the key that would unlock a political problem and make all the pieces fit together. But there was no such key to the Brown problem, and no neat solution. There were only more or less unpalatable alternatives, each of them ugly and uncertain, with plenty of loose ends. Domestic politics is hard work because there are no levers to pull to get things to go your way. There is simply the political grind. Bill Clinton loved the grind. Blair was close to Clinton and saw him as a kind of mentor. Yet in many ways they were opposites. Blair liked to do what Clinton couldn't: he was endlessly searching for the bigger picture beyond the messy details. But he failed to manage what came naturally to Clinton: keeping one step ahead of his rivals. As a result he gravitated naturally towards foreign affairs, where the big-picture politician can feel truly at home. In domestic politics he often reached for wishful solutions that had no chance of success because he hadn't thought hard enough about what might happen next.

This emerges most clearly not from Blair's memoirs but from Peter Mandelson's, which give a much more complete account of the tortured Blair/Brown relationship. Mandelson reveals that Blair frequently pledged to 'do something' about Gordon, only to shy away when the moment came to act. Finally, in the summer of 2003, he commissioned Mandelson to draw up a plan to neutralise Brown's malign influence by splitting the Treasury in two: on the one hand, a reduced Ministry of Finance, restricted to matters of macroeconomics with Brown still in charge; then a separate Office of Budget and Delivery, which would be placed in the Cabinet Office and subject to control from Number Ten, and would deal with all government funding and spending. They christened this plan Operation Teddy Bear. As you read about it, you immediately think: there is no way Gordon is going to agree to this. Then you think: they must have known that, so the plan must include a strategy for dealing with Brown's refusal to accept it. But Blair has no such strategy. After months of dithering he takes the plan to Brown, who responds with a flat 'No'. At which point Blair decides it would be too dangerous to proceed, and shelves it.

Instead, he agrees to a catastrophic deal, brokered by John Prescott, which commits him to handing over to Brown before the end of his second term, on the condition that Brown gives him his full support in the interim. As even Blair acknowledges, this was a terrible mistake. The agreement made no sense, because its terms were entirely unequal – it was asymmetric warfare. Whether Blair kept his side of the bargain was an unarguable matter of fact, whereas Brown's honouring his commitment was always going to be a matter of opinion. When Blair reneges a year later, and pledges to stand again in 2005 for a full third term, Brown, of course, feels betrayed, insisting he has offered the government his full support and Tony has simply shafted him. He becomes more or less unmanageable from this point on, until he finally succeeds in driving Blair from office in 2007. In the end, then, Brown could not be contained.

⁙

Blair himself draws no direct connection between his handling of Brown and his approach to foreign policy. But the connection is clear from Mandelson's account. The war on terror was a means of escape from the hand-to-hand combat of his confrontation with his neighbour in Downing Street. Mandelson says that Blair first began to despair of his relationship with Brown as early as the summer of 2001, shortly after Labour had been re-elected to a second term with another huge majority. This should have been the moment for Blair to press ahead with New Labour reforms of the public services, but he is worried that Brown stands in the way. He tells Mandelson that he is going to take Brown on, that he is tired of being pushed around. But behind all the big talk nothing happens, because Blair does not have the stomach for the fight. Then, on the evening of 11 September 2001, Mandelson encounters a different Blair entirely, no longer angry and exasperated, but exuding 'a resolute sense of calm'. It is hard to avoid the conclusion that Blair is relieved: here at last is a kind of politics that suits his intellectual temperament, far removed from all the intractable difficulties of his relationship with Brown. In his own memoir Blair strongly reinforces the impression that 9/11 was a moment not of terror but of liberation. Watching the plane hit the second tower, from his hotel room in Blackpool just before he was due to address a hostile TUC Conference, he realises this is an attack, not an accident. At that moment, he writes:

> I felt eerily calm despite being naturally horrified at the devastation [...] At one level, it was a shock, a seemingly senseless act of evil. At another level, it made sense of developments I had seen growing in the world these past years – isolated acts of terrorism, disputes marked by the same elements of extremism, and a growing strain of

religious ideology that was always threatening to erupt, and now had.

Within a short space of time, it was clear the casualties would be measured in thousands. I ordered my thoughts. It was the worst terrorist attack in human history. It was not America alone who was the target, but all of us who shared the same values. We had to stand together. We had to understand the scale of the challenge and rise to meet it. We could not give up until it was done. Unchecked and unchallenged, this could threaten our way of life to its fundamentals. There was no other course; no other option; no alternative path. It was war.

All this, Blair says, came to him in the forty minutes between the first attack and the moment he had to tell the TUC that he would not be delivering his speech. 'And it came with total clarity. Essentially, it stayed with that clarity and stays still, in the same way, as clear now as it was then.'

Less than three weeks after the attacks Blair delivered his famous speech to the Labour Party Conference in which he said: 'The kaleidoscope has been shaken. The pieces are in flux. Soon they will settle again. Before they do, let us reorder this world around us.' It was, in his own words, a 'visionary' speech, and he wrote it all himself, in the study overlooking the Rose Garden at Chequers, a single draft composed with little hesitation and no agonising. While he wrote it, he picked up from the desk a silver and gold inkstand given to Chamberlain in 1937, with an inscription that reads: 'To stand on the ancient ways, to see which is the right and the good way, and in that to walk.' (Really someone should go around removing these objects from Chequers before the more impressionable prime ministers move in.) In the speech, Blair went out of his way to link the war on terror with everything else he believed in. 'This is a fight for freedom,' he told his audience.

And I mean: freedom, not only in the narrow sense of
personal liberty, but in the broader sense of each individual having the economic and social freedom to develop
their potential to the full. That is what community
means, founded on the equal worth of all. The starving,
the wretched, the dispossessed, the ignorant, those living
in want and squalor from the deserts of Northern Africa
to the slums of Gaza to the mountain ranges of Afghanistan: they too are our cause.

So this is what Blair means by digging down: you look for
something that will let you join up all the dots. And when you
have found it, you do not let it go.

In fact, Blair had been here before. In 1993, as Labour's
relatively new shadow home secretary, he gave a speech in
response to the shocking murder by two ten-year-olds of the
toddler James Bulger that brought him to national promin-
ence, and served as a kind of template for his response to
9/11. The Bulger murder, Blair believed, in its depravity and its
horror, served to make the connection between other, lesser
crimes that might otherwise go unnoticed. 'The headlines
shock,' he said, 'but what shocks us more is our knowledge
that in almost every city, town or village more minor versions
of the same events are becoming an almost everyday part of
our lives. These are the ugly manifestations of a society that
is becoming unworthy of that name.' The isolated killing of
one small boy explained the condition of Britain; as a result, it
didn't need explaining on its own terms. The Bulger case also
served the useful function of helping Blair to come out from
the shadow of Gordon Brown. Until that point Brown had
been the dominant member of the partnership. (It had even
been Brown who supplied Blair with what was to become his
catch-phrase: 'Tough on crime, tough on the causes of crime.')
But Blair's Bulger speech gave him a different status, as a big-
picture politician, unafraid to draw moral lessons, while Brown

was still known for grappling with the nuts and bolts of tax-and-spend. Blair's approach was lapped up by the tabloids, which started to see him as possibly one of their own. The analysis supplied by the speech was wrong – this one murder did not reveal anything about the true state of British society, only at best something about some small part of it – but that was neither here nor there. Blair had found a way to make it all fit together.

His analysis of 9/11 was also wrong, with much farther-reaching consequences. The attack was an act of deliberate provocation, designed to draw the West into war, and Western politicians had a real choice after it happened: they could have chosen not to be provoked. But for Blair going down that route would have meant simply 'managing' the problem, instead of confronting it. It would also have meant disaggregating the threat of global terrorism into its component parts, rather than seeing it as part of a greater whole. Blair can't bring himself to do that. The same pattern repeats itself when Blair is faced with another crisis later in his premiership, the Israel–Lebanon war of 2006. Again, he acknowledges that Hizbullah firing rockets on Israel was 'a quite deliberate provocation' and that 'Israel reacted to the provocation in the way that it does': with total force. But he cannot agree with those who regard the Israeli response as counter-productive or an over-reaction, because that would be to miss the bigger picture. 'By now,' he writes, 'I had come to see the entire conventional approach in dealing with this problem as itself part of the problem.' So what was the real problem?

> To most people, in July 2006, looking at the news it was the Israel/Lebanon conflict. I didn't see it like that. I defined the problem as the wider struggle between the strain of religious extremism in Islam and the rest of us. To me, Lebanon was embroiled in something far bigger and more portentous than a temporary fight with Israel.

Indeed, I thought the whole issue of Israel part of the broader picture.

By refusing to criticise Israel, Blair did himself immense damage with his colleagues in the Labour Party, and almost certainly hastened the end of his premiership. But by this point he would rather give up being prime minister than give up on his holistic vision of global politics.

||||

Blair is kidding himself if he thinks his intellectual approach to the world's problems has much in common with the forensic legal techniques of a barrister like Derry Irvine. It seems more likely that it stems from the influence of his other great mentor and guide when a young man, the Australian priest Peter Thomson, who became Blair's closest friend and confidant while he was an undergraduate at Oxford. When Thomson died, in 2010, Blair said at his funeral: 'There are few people of whom you can say: he changed my life. Peter changed mine [...] He shaped my life, gave it meaning and purpose, and set its course.' Thomson persuaded Blair that the only way to think about politics was to start with a view of humankind grounded in religion. As Blair puts it: 'I begin with an analysis of human beings as my compass; the politics is secondary.' Thomson also introduced the young Blair to the works of the Scottish philosopher John Macmurray, who became something of a cult for the two of them and a few others at Oxford. (Thomson liked to refer to Macmurray's writings as simply 'the Stuff'.) Macmurray's philosophy committed his disciples to seeing linkages everywhere: between individuals and communities, between rights and obligations and, above all, between words and actions. This last was very important for Thomson, whom Blair describes as 'a doer not a spectator, and a thinker not just a preacher': 'His Christianity was muscular, not limp.'

The charge of being a preachy politician is one that has always irked Blair intensely. (Dick Cheney's jibe about 'that preacher on a tank' must really have stung.) Macmurray ended his life as a Quaker, so it is unlikely that Blair got his taste for military action from that source. But Thomson's example may account for another leitmotif of Blair's personal philosophy and of this memoir: his obsession with what he calls 'grip'. Faced with a challenge, Blair believes you have to do two things: first, you think it through; then you grip it. Merely 'managing' it is never enough.

The importance of grip was driven home for Blair at various critical moments in his premiership before 9/11. One came during the winter of 2000–01, when he faced a pair of domestic crises. The first was the fuel protests of September 2000, when blockades of refining plants in protest at rising petrol prices threatened to bring the country to a halt. Blair describes the rising panic in his inner circle – and in his own mind – about what could be done to prevent the chaos, until he decides to take a grip on the problem personally. He announces to a group of oil executives and police officers that he wants the picket lines broken up; if that provokes violence from the protesters, 'let the army take care of them'. The police like the sound of this, the oil executives don't, until Blair makes some vaguely threatening remarks about mounting public anger at their excessive profits, at which point they start to get a hold of themselves. 'I ended the meeting,' Blair says, 'satisfied we were at least gripping it and beginning the process of turning things around.'

The second crisis began in February 2001, with the discovery of foot-and-mouth at a farm in Essex. Before long, the disease had spread around the country, which meant a ban on British meat exports and the closing down of large parts of the countryside. Tackling the disease was the responsibility of the Ministry of Agriculture and its secretary of state, Nick Brown, who happened to be one of Gordon Brown's closest allies (though no relation). Blair says he did not want to interfere but became increasingly alarmed at Brown's failure to get a grip. So he decided to do it himself. 'There was pain, panic and real grief out there,' he recalls. 'The only answer was slaughter, and the only way to do it was fast.' He goes on:

> The challenge was how to do it. We could throw resources at it, but throw them where? At the weekend, I got down to Chequers early. It always helped me clear my head. I read all the papers, spoke to a few people. The chief vet Jim Scudamore was a good bloke, but he was overwhelmed. We all were. I got as detailed a briefing as I could. Then I just sat and thought.

On his return to Downing Street on Sunday, Blair concludes he has no choice but 'to grip the whole thing'. He gathers his close advisers, who in this case include his chief scientific adviser, David King. King explains to him what needs to be done. 'Essentially, by means of graphs and charts he set out how the disease would spread, how we could contain it if we took the right culling measures, and how over time we would eradicate it.' Blair was sceptical: 'How could he predict it like that, with so many unknowns? But, almost faute de mieux, I followed his advice – and blow me, with uncanny, almost unnatural accuracy, the disease peaked, declined and went, almost to the week he had predicted.'

But that is not the whole story. What Blair leaves out is that, in this case too, he was only able to deal with the problem by calling on the armed forces, who took charge of the cull once it was clear that the Ministry of Agriculture's resources were overstretched. I was struck at the time by how efficiently the operation moved once Blair had decided to call in the troops, and I wondered what conclusions Blair would draw from this about the best ways to achieve 'delivery', given his obviously growing frustrations with the civil service and with the Treasury. Blair reveals that his chief of staff, Jonathan Powell, overheard a phone conversation at the height of the crisis between the two Browns, during which Gordon warned Nick not to give in to Blair's 'presidential style'. It is a cliché of the Blair years, and not really true, that his was a presidential premiership: had it been, he could have fired Brown without having to worry so much about the consequences. But in this respect the warning seems prescient. Even on his own account, for all his pose as a solitary thinker, Blair didn't really grip the problem of foot-and-mouth himself: he found an adviser who was able to tell him what to do, and who made all the unknowns magically disappear. What Blair did do, however, was behave like a commander-in-chief.

The other place where Blair exercised his personal grip was in Northern Ireland, during the negotiations that secured the Good Friday agreement in April 1998. This is when Blair's strengths – along with some of Clinton's – really came together to make the crucial difference. There is no doubt that Blair's determination and charm played a big part in getting the parties to sign up to something that just a few years earlier would have seemed impossible. Indeed, Blair was told on his arrival at Stormont, where the discussions were to take place, that a deal was 'a non-starter' and 'undoable'. 'I took the decision then and there,' he says, 'to take complete charge of the negotiation.' He mastered the detail, found the common ground, fudged the points of irreconcilable difference and kept all sides from walking away in their moments of despair or disgust, until, exhausted after four days of non-stop talking, everyone signed up to an agreement it was far from clear that anyone really understood. It was a great achievement. But Blair is on far shakier ground when he says it is possible to extract from his experiences in Northern Ireland 'core principles that have a general application' to cases of conflict resolution around the world. His first principle is, predictably, 'to go back to first principles' and ask: 'What is it really about? What are we trying to achieve? What is at the heart of the matter?' The second principle is:

> To proceed to resolution, the thing needs to be gripped and focused on. Continually. Inexhaustibly. Relentlessly. Day by day by day by day. The biggest problem with the Middle East peace process is that no one has ever gripped it long enough or firmly enough. The gripping is intermittent, and intermittent won't do. It doesn't work. If it was gripped, it would be solved.

It sounds too good to be true, and it is. It also makes you wonder why Blair – once his premiership was over – only ever worked part-time as a peace envoy to the Middle East, fitting it in between his other, more lucrative activities, rather than focusing on it day by day by day by day. What Blair doesn't sufficiently acknowledge is that Northern Ireland wasn't solved because he was able to grip it, but that he was able to grip it because it was ready to be solved. The circumstances were right, including, as Blair concedes, the economic circumstances. Northern Ireland was now affluent enough to make peace a more attractive option than war. Moreover, there was relative economic parity between the North and the South for the first time in their history. (This is where any analogy with the Middle East starts to break down.) Of course, the politicians still had to make it work. As Blair says, 'Leaders matter.' By that he is referring not only to himself but also to the leaders of all the main parties. He concludes: 'We were very lucky in the quality of leadership we had.' Indeed, on his account, everyone was heroic: David Trimble, Ian Paisley, Gerry Adams, Martin McGuinness, Bertie Ahern, John Hume, even Seamus Mallon and Mark Durkan of the SDLP and David Ervine of the Progressive Unionist Party. This also seems too good to be true. Was this really the golden age of Irish politics, akin to the United States in 1776, when a group of supremely talented individuals took destiny into their own hands? Or was it that they all could see the time was right to strike a deal? What is really remarkable is how often they kept coming back to the table, when it would seem to be easier to walk away. In the end, you have to conclude that walking away was the tougher option. This is not to downplay Blair's role in holding the whole thing together. But his experiences in Northern Ireland were never going to be the key that would unlock peace around the world.

Blair's mistake after 9/11 was to try to grip things that were not grippable, certainly not by him. First in Afghanistan, then in Iraq, he vastly overestimated his ability to control what would happen. There were far too many unknowns, and nothing he or his experts could do to magic them away. Moreover, these weren't his wars, they were America's, and they were going to happen with him or without him. In those circumstances, his ability to exert any sort of grip was negligible. It is true that he had set the terms for American military action once before, in Kosovo, when he took the lead in pressing for a ground invasion to drive Milošević out. In the end, Bill Clinton reluctantly agreed to back up Blair's words with the threat of American military muscle, and Milošević backed down. But Kosovo is not Iraq, any more than Northern Ireland is the Middle East. And George W. Bush was not Clinton. Blair makes a great deal of the closeness of his relationship with Bush, and describes how Bush regularly consulted with him and consistently impressed him with his grasp of the big issues. Yet he supplies no evidence that Bush ever actually listened to what he was saying or followed his advice. He tells us that in the run-up to the invasion of Afghanistan, he gave Bush the full benefit of his wisdom:

> I was writing regular notes to him, raising issues, prompting his system and mine: humanitarian aid; political alliances, including in particular how we co-opted the Northern Alliance (the anti-Taliban coalition) without

giving the leadership of the country over to them; economic development; reconciliation in the aftermath of a
hopefully successful military operation.

This is designed to give the impression of a fully hands-on
leader. But it sounds more like someone who has lost his grip
on political reality.

|||||

Blair had reached the limits of his power. The person his
behaviour at this juncture brings to mind is another man who
had grown frustrated with not being king. Prince Charles
spent Blair's premiership writing him and his ministers regular
notes, full of his own advice and promptings. Receiving
Charles's handwritten letters, as Blair explains, was an occupa-
tional hazard of being prime minister. They had to be politely
acknowledged, but could be just as politely ignored. Blair treats
Charles in much the way one imagines Bush treated him: half
respectfully, half mockingly. He respects Charles's sincerity,
but pities his lack of political nous. The royal Blair really connected with was Princess Diana, about whom he writes at
some length. Diana, he felt, had it all: not just the charm and
the looks, but 'a strong emotional intelligence' and 'analytical
understanding'. Indeed, she showed a mind 'that was not only
intuitive but also had a really good process of reasoning'. All in
all, she was a natural politician. 'I always used to say to Alastair
[Campbell]: if she were ever in politics, even Clinton would
have to watch out.' Here Blair is truly kidding himself. He
admits, in the jaunty and laddish tone he likes to adopt when
talking about his life outside politics, 'I really liked her and,
of course, was as big a sucker for a beautiful princess as the
next man.' But Diana was far too feckless and self-indulgent for
politics. The would-be politician was Charles, who is more like
Blair than either of them might care to admit. They share the

same intellectual ambition, a taste for holistic philosophy and a sense of themselves as deep thinkers. Of course, the difference as Blair sees it is that Charles hasn't really got any 'grip'. So they shared some of the same illusions as well.

Charles has made it clear that when he becomes king he will have to pipe down, because he knows that being in the top job means he has to be careful about being seen to go too far. For Blair, the reverse was true: the closer he came to the end of his time at the top, the more determined he was to speak out. He won the 2005 election, but only by default, against a still toxic Conservative Party, and one that lacked the guts to challenge him over Iraq. By this point, he admits, he had more or less ceded all control of economic matters to Gordon Brown – an admission that is designed in part to lumber Brown with the blame for not tackling the underlying problems that came to a head in the 2007/8 financial crisis (conveniently just after Blair left office). At the same time, though, Blair felt that he was finally starting to master the job of prime minister. He now knows what he wants to do and is no longer afraid of going out on a limb to achieve it. Only Gordon stands in the way, demanding that he begin the process of arranging an 'orderly transition'. Blair is therefore deeply impressed by a letter he gets from his adviser Andrew Adonis, setting this predicament in historical context.

1.   There are no 'dignified exits' and 'orderly transitions' – just exits and transitions, all more or less ragged and unsatisfactory. That's life, I suppose.

2.   The more successful prime ministers all left Number Ten with the least 'dignified' and most 'disorderly' transitions. Gladstone, Lloyd George, Churchill, Macmillan and Thatcher all possessed a will to power for a purpose until the very end [...] By contrast, the three long-serving prime ministers to execute 'dignified' and 'orderly' transitions

> are Wilson, Baldwin and Salisbury – all drained of energy and purpose, their reputations and uniformly disastrous legacies not enhanced by the warm retirement tributes.

Blair is inspired by this to stand and fight. He tells a newspaper that he has no plans to set an exit date. When the interview appears, it so enrages Brown and his supporters that they effectively seize the moment to drive Blair from office, forcing him within a week to agree that he will be gone by the following summer. So the effect of Adonis's advice, and of Blair's characteristic lack of political calculation, is exactly the opposite of what was intended. He spends the remaining months of his premiership giving ever more ambitious speeches setting out his political philosophy, to ever diminishing returns. No one is really listening any more. But as Adonis predicted, he received plenty of retirement tributes when the moment finally arrived, including a standing ovation in the House of Commons following his final appearance at Prime Minister's Questions.

I once asked someone who was close to the Blair project in its heyday if he could define the essential core of Blairism, beyond the grand schemes and foreign adventures. He said it was simple: the guiding principle was that 'Gordon Brown must not become prime minister'. So the project ultimately failed in its own terms. Blair was succeeded by a politician who had been his long-standing friend before turning into his implacable enemy. He conveys his sense of betrayal by castigating Brown for having moved away from the ideas they both once believed in. Ultimately, Blair blames Brown for departing from the New Labour template of public service reform, an emphasis on crime and anti-social behaviour and a rigorous avoidance of direct tax rises, and he blames Brown's defeat in the 2010 general election on this refusal to stick to the Blair agenda. He thinks the economic crisis was a missed opportunity for the government to reassert its New Labour credentials: instead of showing that it was serious about paring back the deficit and making the state more efficient, it retreated into its Keynesian comfort zone. In the end, Blair was clearly much more comfortable with the politics of the coalition government than those of the Labour government it replaced. The leaders of the coalition were also much more comfortable with him. David Cameron and his then ally Michael Gove used to refer to Blair in private as 'the Master', and his memoirs became required reading for their inner circle. 'What Would Tony Do?' became something of a mantra for the Cameroons. Yet this generation of acolytes has also let the master down badly. Ultimately, they gave us Brexit, which is the last thing Tony would have done.

That raises a question that has often been asked of Blair: was he really a Conservative underneath? He is aware of the charge and he denies it, saying that the Tories never really get the bigger picture. 'Their policies will be skewed towards those at the top, fashioned too much by the preoccupations of the elite (which is why they despised action on anti-social behaviour) and too conservative, particularly in foreign policy.' So: not tough enough on crime, too reluctant to use armed force abroad – an odd way to defend yourself against the charge of dressing to the right! But the real problem is that the Tories lack the right values and, above all, a consistent commitment to social justice. Blair bemoans the lurch towards blind partisanship that has taken place since his time in office, and he insists that many policies traditionally associated with the right are the ones progressives should support: 'Defining where you stand by reference to the opposite of where the other person stands is not just childish, it is completely out of touch with where politics is today.' Given where politics is today, that sounds like an increasingly plaintive cry. But even Blair thinks there is a fundamental difference between his worldview and that of the other side. What the Tories cannot manage is to join up the dots. When they do the right thing, it is just by chance. When Blair does the right thing, he still believes, it is because he has drilled down.

5

GORDON BROWN

GORDON BROWN WANTS us to know what it was actually like to be right in the middle of the drama of his prime minister-ship. It's a noble aim. Given his rollercoaster tenure in Downing Street, punctuated by the gut-wrenching twists and turns of the financial crisis, there should have been plenty of stand-out moments to choose from. Some, though, were already taken. Alistair Darling, for instance, starts *Back from the Brink*, his 2011 account of the fraught period he served as Brown's chancellor, on Tuesday, 7 October 2008, when Sir Tom McKillop, the chairman of RBS, called him to announce that his bank was about to go bust and to ask what the government planned to do about it. 'It was going to be a bad day,' Darling says with dry understatement. Brown adopts a different approach in his memoirs. His starting point is Friday, 8 May 2009. He picks it because it was an ordinary day in the life of a prime minister and he wants us to see how extraordinary that is.

His day starts at 5 a.m., with a spell on the Downing Street treadmill, before arriving at his desk to work on two important speeches he has to give the following week. He went to bed the night before after being told of the death of a British soldier in Afghanistan; now over breakfast he is informed of the deaths of three more servicemen there in a suicide bombing. 'I felt nauseous,' he writes. 'I thought of the families across Britain

[...] who were about to receive a visit; of the moment when the doorbell rings and they already sense the terrible news they are about to be told.' He does not have long to dwell on this, however. His morning gets worse when he opens the *Daily Telegraph*. He is already embroiled in a dispute with the paper over what he sees as its malicious misreporting of his expenses claims. Now he discovers that there is an article by one of his predecessors, John Major, that attacks him in highly personal terms. He decides he must ring the *Telegraph*'s editor to put the record straight. He has to do this on a train to Bradford, where he is due to unveil a memorial in honour of a local police officer, Sharon Beshenivsky, who was murdered in an armed robbery four years earlier. When the call to the *Telegraph* comes through, he ends up taking it 'in the cramped space between two carriages that were bouncing up and down as passengers squeezed by on their way to the buffet bar'.

After Bradford it's on to Sheffield, where he performs the opening ceremonies for a new academy school and a Sure Start centre, before a visit to a struggling steel business. On the journey home he gets embroiled in an email exchange with one of his advisers on the never-ending challenge of trying to nail down the peace in Northern Ireland. He also feels he has to respond to an email from the actress Joanna Lumley, badgering him about rights of residence for Gurkhas living in the UK. Back in London he takes calls from foreign leaders about the continuing fall-out from the financial crisis, grapples with some of the complexities of the Calman Commission on extending the powers of the Scottish Parliament and hosts a strategy session on the forthcoming local and European elections. Before he goes to bed, his speechwriter Kirsty McNeill sends him a copy of a poem to perk him up. It pays tribute to the American baseball star Ted Williams: 'Watch the ball and do your thing/ This is the moment. Here's your chance/ Don't let anyone mess with your swing.' Brown responds gratefully: 'Brilliant poem. We need a British version of it.'

Brown feels this picture should be enough to give a sense of the unique challenge of being prime minister in the age of 24/7 media communication, facing 'a weight and breadth of issues that is difficult to comprehend, yet alone control, and a speed at which you have to work and make decisions that almost defies belief'. No one can understand it fully who hasn't done it. Well, yes and no. Of course, it's hard to imagine what it would be like to be told as a regular part of your job that people are dying on your watch. That has always been part of the unique and fearsome challenge of national political leadership. But the rest of it – the lack of headspace, the intrusion of issues that you thought were done for now, the fire-fighting, the press of voices demanding attention – sounds more like the life of any overworked professional in the twenty-first century. We've all been there, squeezing out a call in the jostle of the crowded train, wondering whether there'll ever be time to sit down, never mind wind down. Brown harks back to the age when prime ministers had the leisure to read poetry (Disraeli and Gladstone), write love letters (Asquith) or take morning drinks and afternoon naps (Churchill). No doubt there are lawyers, doctors, accountants, even writers, who feel the same sense of nostalgia for a rhythm of life that's never coming back. Though he clearly regrets how relentless it was, Brown wants us to know he wasn't undone by the clamour and that, despite all the demands, he managed to cope. Indeed, he did more than cope – he thrived. He calls himself 'the first email prime minister'. Welcome to our world, Gordon.

There is therefore something strangely solipsistic about the way Brown insists that his first-hand political experiences give him a unique perspective into what was really happening. Often he sounds just like everyone else, without quite realising it. Writing about his experiences in the 1992 election, when Labour under Neil Kinnock snatched defeat from the jaws of victory, he says:

For me, two images stand out from the last few days of the campaign: on the one hand, John Major on a simple wooden soapbox making his final campaign speeches; on the other, Labour's big-budget triumphalist Sheffield rally that resembled a US-style political convention. With ten thousand party members in attendance, Neil's human and emotional response to the adoring crowd – 'We're alright! We're alright! We're alright!' – came under fire from the right-wing press.

That 'For me ...', with its promise of some special insight, is truly bizarre, given what follows. Those are the only two things anyone can remember about that campaign – they are what it's known for! It's as though he was watching it on TV like everyone else, rather than being a part of the action. By contrast, it's at the moments when Brown wants to show us his human side – to let us see that he has his fair share of frailties – that he sounds most different from other people. Then there is something missing, an empty space where the real person should be.

||||
||||

Brown considers his greatest failing as prime minister was his inability to communicate effectively. It is what politicians who find themselves out of their depth often believe. He thinks he was on top of the rest of the demands of political leadership: the mastery of detail, the hard work, a commitment to the cause and a passionate conviction about what needed to be done. What he lacked was the capacity to bring the British people along with him when he needed them. He would get the policy right, but in his own words that was often at the expense of 'getting the message across'. As he led the country out of the financial crisis that gripped the world in 2008, this gap was his undoing. 'My own biggest regret was that in the greatest peacetime challenge – a catastrophic global recession that threatened to become a depression – I failed to persuade the British people that the progressive policies I pushed for, nationally and internationally, were the right and fairest way to respond.'

So determined is he to push the message that communication was his one real weakness that his sense of regret sometimes spills over into absurd levels of self-chastisement. The first email prime minister never got the hang of Twitter, and now he feels that this was very negligent. He notes that Margaret Thatcher did all right without it – indeed, he says, 'the very idea that she could have contained her thoughts to 140 [or even 280] characters is preposterous. The Lady was not for tweeting. But I should have been.' Really? Not only is it hard to see how Twitter would have helped in the dark days of the financial crisis; this is also a piece of historical revisionism. Twitter only got going in 2007, the year Brown became prime minister. Given how busy he was, it would have taken some special prescience to think of this as his means of winning over the public, especially since many of them had as little idea of what Twitter was as he did. 'During my time as an MP,' he writes, 'I never mastered the capacity to leave a good impression or sculpt my public image in 140 characters.' As so often in this telling, the real message here is a dig at Blair. Unlike Brown, Blair never even mastered email – he got his staff to type up his electronic communications for him – which left him free to indulge his taste for superficial theatrics. Lucky old Tony didn't have to grapple with his inbox night and day. If only Gordon had been less diligent in dealing with the issues as they arose, he might have had time to tweet his way out of trouble.

On Brown's account, the central challenge in politics comes from the tension between policy and presentation, with the prize going to the person who can master both. By implication, Blair was presentation without the policy, whereas with Brown it was the other way round – preferable, though still not enough. But this analysis won't do. It leaves out the thing that makes politics politics. Along with policy and presentation there is power or, to put it more bluntly, brute force. Sometimes, in order to get people to do what you want, it is necessary to coerce them. Brown does not want to talk about this. It isn't that he denies that it happens. He describes plenty of moments when people use methods of communication to bully, threaten and coerce, rather than to persuade. It's just that when this happens, it is being done to him. It is never being done by him.

His main grievance is against the Murdoch press, which hounded him during the latter part of his tenure as chancellor and throughout his time as prime minister. Some of this also relates to his struggles with Blair. When John Smith died in 1994, and Brown reluctantly decided to step aside to allow Blair to take the crown, it was partly because 'the Murdoch press were all backing Tony [...] writing [him] up as the only moderniser. It was wholly unfair but predictable.' Brown feared that if he took Blair on he would give the papers an excuse to lambast him as the anti-moderniser and to present Labour as split. But their later persecution of him went well beyond stirring up internal party divisions. It was deeply personal and it was also, as Brown puts it, 'overtly political'. His tax returns were stolen, his medical records were hacked, police officers were bribed for access to the details they held on him. *The Sun* in particular, under the editorship of Rebekah Brooks, made repeated intrusions into his private life in order to get him on the back foot. Brown calls it 'a direct attempt to distort and suborn the policy of the government'. He accepts that the Tory press was always likely to be hostile, and that criticism of his policy positions was inevitable. What he cannot accept is that they used such strong-arm methods to try to get their way. This was not an attempt to communicate an alternative point of view. It was simply bullying.

But it wasn't just the press. Someone else who Brown

felt had a habit of playing dirty when he should have known better was the governor of the Bank of England, Mervyn King. Throughout the financial crisis Brown believed that King went beyond his remit in permitting his political views – particularly what Brown calls 'his personal attitude to debt' – to interfere with his policy role. He allowed himself to become a 'public commentator', he 'pontificated', he was 'excessively political'. King repeated the offence in 2010, when he gave advice to the Liberal Democrats during the coalition negotiations that clearly favoured the Tory position on the urgency of adopting an austerity programme. 'Mervyn King,' Brown writes, 'failed to understand the limits of his unelected position.' His job as governor was to provide factual advice in relation to fiscal matters. He ended up pushing for a particular course of action, based on exaggerated claims of what might happen if it was not followed. It was not exactly bullying, but it did come in the form of a threat – do this, or the economy gets it.

Brown's complaints seem entirely justified. The behaviour of the Murdoch press was monstrous. The Bank of England under King did have ideas above its station. Brown certainly had a much better financial crisis than the Bank did. But what will not wash is the other side of the story: Brown's suggestion that he never fought back in kind. He says nothing about how he responded to press intrusion or attempts by unelected officials to stray into his territory. Indeed, he goes out of his way to say that 'I did not do a Harold Wilson and publicly criticise Mervyn, even when on further occasions he volunteered advice on our fiscal policy.' All he will say is that he called him in for a private chat, and reminded him of their understanding 'that I would not comment on monetary policy and he would refrain from weighing in on fiscal policy'. As a result, 'Mervyn promised not to intervene again.' Then, three months later, he went back on his word. Policy and promises, either kept or broken. That, according to this account, is all politics is.

As a result, the picture Brown presents is full of gaping

holes where the actual politics should be. Repeatedly Brown's descriptions of key events make little sense because he doesn't give us so much as a hint of the coercive menace that lay behind them. For instance, he describes the Blair government's response to the fuel blockade in 2000 as a victory for his principled position that 'whatever we did had to be justifiable on wider policy grounds'. He makes no mention of Blair's threat to deploy the army, or the fear that gripped the government when the situation seemed to be running out of control, or the fact that both the Blair and Brown camps saw the management of the crisis as a proxy for the ongoing battle between them. Brown's discussion of his own decision in 2007 to shirk a general election, which gave him a reputation for cowardice he was never able to shake off, is presented as another accident of miscommunication. He was, he says, too busy with the policy challenges he faced in his early days as prime minister to pay much attention to the question of whether he could beat the Tories in a snap election. 'I was handed some polling,' he recalls, 'but because I was not planning an election I did not study it in any detail.' If you believe that, you'll believe anything. If Brown now believes it, then he no longer knows who he really is. It's as though the central motif of his political career – his ability to look for weakness on the other side and exploit it – was simply an invention of the dishonest media. He takes full responsibility for his failure to dampen down the speculation that an election might be coming, but again this is held up as evidence of his being preoccupied with substance when a more adept politician might have paid more attention to the froth. The thought that battering the Tories into submission was part of his calculations is never entertained.

Perhaps the most jarring example is his description of what happened after Alistair Darling gave an interview to the *Guardian* in August 2007 at the start of the financial crisis, in which he described it as the gravest economic threat facing the country for sixty years. 'He was absolutely right,' Brown says, 'but he wrong-footed us because he was interpreted as singling out a peculiarly British problem. When we later talked by the phone, he and I were agreed that we had to emphasise the reality that the roots and failures were worldwide.' That's it: message squared, policy intact. Compare this to Darling's own account of what happened next:

> It was the briefing machine at Number Ten, and Gordon's attack dogs, who fed the story and kept it running. I later described it as being like 'the forces of hell' being unleashed on me [...] For days after the *Guardian* piece ran, journalists told us they were repeatedly being told that I had made a hash of it [...] At the time, what I didn't know was that [...] Gordon had told journalists that we would see an economic recovery within six months [...] If I had known that Gordon believed that economic recovery lay around the corner – if he'd told me, his chancellor, this – then we could have had a discussion about it. The problem was that he clearly did not trust my advice, and now he appeared indifferent to what I thought [...] Systematic anonymous briefing from people you have known for years, and who are supposed to be on your side, is deeply unpleasant. Living next door to it – literally – was all the harder. I was reminded of the words Henry II uttered about Thomas à Becket: 'Will no one rid me of this turbulent priest.' He didn't order his knights to go and kill Becket, but they believed they had his blessing to do so.

Now that sounds like politics.

||||

There were always two sides to Brown's personality. He was, as he describes, a notably high-minded politician, committed to the cause of social justice. He was interested in big ideas and in the hard graft of turning new thinking into workable policies. Those who worked with him can testify to his genuine commitment to building a better Britain. One senior policy adviser described him to me as truly 'Gladstonian' in his seriousness of purpose. But that same person also said there would be occasions when he would open the door to a meeting between Brown and his political henchmen and realise that he had no business there. In fact, it would be better not to know what was being discussed, because anyone in the room would be compromised by what they heard. This was the other side of Brown: the politician who played as dirty as his opponents, and sometimes even dirtier. Blair wanted the different parts of political life to join up. Brown went out of his way to keep them separate.

It is hardly surprising that Brown is unwilling to discuss his knowledge of the dark arts. He has little to say about his two attack dogs, Damian McBride and Charlie Whelan, the men who terrorised Darling, among many others. McBride nearly destroyed Brown's premiership when he had to resign in 2009 after one dirty trick too far. He gets a minor telling off from Brown for 'repeating gossip that had no basis in fact', but a bigger chit for subsequently writing a 'very honest and penitent book blaming only himself for what he called "the power trip" he had been on'. So that's all right then: it was a personal error of judgement on McBride's part to think that power was the name of the game. Wherever can he have got that impression? His real job was meant to be helping Brown present his policy positions more persuasively. When things go wrong, it's simply because the persuasion didn't work as it should. Of tax credits, which Brown devised partly to aid his project of more extensive and efficient redistribution and partly to make sure the Tories couldn't use taxation as another stick to beat him with, he says 'our problem was not, in the end, a failure of policy [...] as on many other occasions, there was a failure in presentation.' But this doesn't take into account that tax credits were also meant to be a useful weapon in his own political arsenal. The trouble he got into – in his last budget as chancellor in 2007 he cut the basic rate of income tax from 22 per cent to 20 and increased tax credits, paying for the changes by abolishing the starting rate of 10 per cent, which caused many Labour supporters to lose out – came about because he didn't want to give up tax credits as a stick he could use on other people, both inside and outside the Parliamentary Labour Party. Brown writes only that 'the tax issue remained a potent weapon in our opponents' hands,' as though they were playing one game and he was playing another. But they were all playing politics.

One of the running sores in Brown's relationship with Blair was the issue of the euro, which Blair wanted to join – seeing it as a crucial part of his legacy – and Brown didn't. As chancellor, Brown devised five tests that would have to be passed if his doubts were to be overcome. This was an eminently sensible policy position, and Brown was right to stick to it. At one point in 2003 it was floated to him that if he were to soften his stance Tony might be willing to hand over the leadership sooner rather than later. But that wasn't the business Brown was in. 'I was adamant: I would not put what I considered to be the national economic interest second to my own political interest.' Instead, he commissioned a massive Treasury study which showed that four of the five tests hadn't been met. 'The document and its appendices were so heavy that they had to be walked over to Number Ten by Treasury messengers.' Nothing threatening about that. Brown then ensured that all members of the cabinet were supplied with eighteen separate studies of the euro question to 'inform their discussions'. He held meetings with each of them individually to explain what these studies meant. When the cabinet met to resolve the issue on 5 June, it was unanimous in deciding that 'membership of the euro was not right for Britain at this time'. Brown wants us to see that it was simply the weight of evidence that told. But it must have been a pretty bruising experience for those on the receiving end. The weight of evidence can beat you up too.

Brown's refusal to acknowledge that politics sometimes entered into his politics can border on the pathological. He says he was reluctant to nationalise Northern Rock, the bank whose collapse in 2007 was the first warning of the impending financial crisis, because it would have meant a very bad deal for the British taxpayer. He doesn't admit that he was terrified of anything that might look like a reversion to the bad old days of socialism. When he agreed before the 2010 election to take part in the televised leaders' debates, it was because 'I thought it right that the country hear the arguments debated through TV questioning.' He also felt it would help level the playing field, since the Tories had more money to spend on advertising, and this was free publicity. What he won't say is that he was desperate, a long way behind in the polls and willing to roll the dice. Yet that's where he was. At times his desire to avoid creating the impression that he was politically calculating is so calculating as to be excruciating. When he recounts the fateful moment during the 2010 general election campaign when he was caught on mic disparaging a voter in Rochdale called Gillian Duffy, who had pressed him on the question of immigration, he admits: 'I made the mistake of describing Mrs Duffy as a "sort of bigoted woman". It was a remark born of frustration that the next day's media coverage would not be about our policing policies.' Of course, what guaranteed that no one would be talking about his policing policies was the fact that Brown had called a Labour supporter a bigot. His moment of temper cannot have been both cause and effect of the media coverage. What he was really frustrated about was that he was losing the election. But he would never admit that.

It is tempting to look to Brown's upbringing for clues to the origins of this quirk in his character: that despite all his political gifts, his political passion and his political determination, he could never quite own up to what it was that drove him – the pursuit of power. His childhood was unremarkable in many respects. Indeed, it was exceptional only in being so middling: 'A middle-class upbringing in middle Scotland in the middle of the century' is the way he describes it. What made it distinctive, however, was that Scotland back then could be described as 'the most religious country in the world', and Brown's father was a minister. He says little about the impact this had on him and almost nothing about his own religious beliefs. He just took it for granted. A bigger influence seems to have come from being one of three brothers. He was particularly drawn to his older brother, John, who blazed a trail for him in journalism, in the media and in political campaigning. The boys worked together on a student newspaper and in student politics. His younger brother, Andrew, took time out from his own media career to work as an adviser to Gordon when he first became an MP.

These were the relationships he cherished: permanent bonds with people who will look out for you regardless. The ones he mistrusted were those based on happening to find yourself in the right place at the right time: he hated the idea that you had to be in the know to get ahead. Or rather, he hated the idea that others might be in the know while he was in the dark. The formative experience of his early years was the rugby accident that cost him the sight of one eye and nearly left him completely blind. When he originally went to see his GP, it was recommended he go to a private consultant to get it checked out. The doctor in question couldn't see him for five months, and during that time Brown's eye deteriorated beyond the point where surgery would be successful. 'Ironically,' he writes, 'I could have gone right away to an eye consultant at my local hospital; but not knowing my way round the NHS at the time I simply took the advice of the GP who directed me to his consultant friend. It would be the last time I would ever go private.' Brown had learned his lesson. Go to the place where they have to look after you. Make sure you know your way around. And God bless the NHS.

If there is a theme to his early political progress, it is that he sought out bands of brothers with whom he could work and from whom he could draw the support he needed as he took the next step. He found a version of this when working as a producer at Scottish Television ('prompted by ever generous friends Russell Galbraith, Bob Cuddihy and Ken Vass') and again in getting selected as parliamentary candidate for Dunfermline East (thanks to his 'great friend Jim McIntyre' and a group of young shop stewards from the Rosyth dockyard, who 'included Charlie Boyle, Helen Dowie, Jimmy Dyce, Charlie Logan, Margaret Logan, Bert Lumsden, George Manclark, Derek Stubbs, Peter Young and also Alex Falconer'). As this shows, they didn't all have to be men, but usually they were. There is no doubt that Brown tried to re-create these bonds with groups of personal allies throughout his political career, and he often succeeded. His closest colleagues from his time at the Treasury, including Geoffrey Robinson, Ed Balls and Ed Miliband, remained remarkably loyal.

But there was, inevitably, a downside. The higher he rose, the more political these friendships became. Being part of Gordon's band was increasingly a choice that came with costs – it deeply alienated the people who weren't. Moreover, the laddish culture these tight-knit groups engendered was a hostage to fortune, as McBride, among others, discovered. Finally, and crucially, there was one relationship that didn't ultimately work on this fraternal model. Brown's very first friendship in the Commons was with Tony Blair. But it never successfully extended beyond the two of them. And it never gave Brown the support he needed. He provided the leg-up to his friend, not the other way round. He never got over it.

When he writes about Blair, the emotion is still clearly raw. He feels he was jilted. But he doesn't come over like a rejected lover. He sounds like a disappointed older brother.

When you are surrounded by people on whom you can instinctively rely, it is easier to imagine that politics is primarily about loyalty, not coercion. If some of them go too far in making the case for the things you believe, well maybe that's just enthusiasm, not malice. Brown is very conscious that something needs to supply the enthusiasm in politics, in a world where religion no longer does. It is striking, for all his angst about Twitter and 24/7 news cycles, that the biggest change he observes over his lifetime is 'the scale and speed of the collapse in religious adherence'. He quotes the philosopher Charles Taylor, who argues that we now live in a world where 'faith, even for the staunchest believer, is one human possibility among others'. Brown also cites with approval John Rawls's notion of the 'overlapping consensus'. He summarises it as follows:

> No matter how strongly felt your religious beliefs, you cannot justify your case for action purely on the grounds of faith, and you have to accept that your views are more likely to command authority in the eyes of non-believers because they are supported by logic, evidence and an appeal to shared values [...] You have to argue your case in the public square, submit to scrutiny, acknowledge alternative points of view – and live with the outcome even if your point of view loses out.

It's another noble ideal. But as Rawls's critics have never tired of pointing out, it leaves out the coercive aspect of politics, which is what makes the public square possible in the first place. Rawls was also a philosopher, so if he wanted to leave out the dark side of politics, that was his business. But Brown was prime minister. And however hard he tried to persuade himself that he was living up to this ideal, he didn't manage it.

There are times when the pursuit of consensus is not what the political occasion demands. The great test of Brown's career was the financial crisis, and it brought out his true qualities as a politician. These were not his powers of reasonable persuasion. They were his grit, his forcefulness and, frankly, his ingrained suspicion that other people might be taking him for a ride. In this case, a paranoid prime minister was just what was needed, because it was the banks' attempt to bury the bad news on their balance sheets that threatened to crash the whole system. Once Brown got past his hope that things might be turned around in six months, he started rattling the bankers' cages to find out what they were hiding. When they told him their problems were merely ones of liquidity, he refused to believe them. He insisted that the real problems were structural. If they needed a name for it, he had one: 'Greed'. Brown saw early on that he would have to be blunt: NO LIQUIDITY WITHOUT RECAPITALISATION was the message he wrote on a memo in his thick felt-tip pen. As he says: 'It didn't have the elegance of "No taxation without representation", but it would do.' It was Brown who got his fellow world leaders to recognise that it would take a huge concerted effort to stave off disaster. When he gathered the members of the G20 for an emergency meeting in London in April 2009, Nicolas Sarkozy complained that the global economy was still in meltdown and 'none of us has a plan'. 'Gordon has a plan,' Obama chipped in helpfully. The rest of them followed it, not because Brown reasoned them round, but because by this point they were as scared shitless as he was.

To Brown's great frustration, though he could get his fellow leaders to sign up to an emergency rescue for the banking system, he couldn't get them to address the structural problems that lay behind the crisis. He had hoped this would be the first step in a concerted international effort to tackle global poverty, climate change and other deep-seated challenges. But in the global public square, once the fear had dissipated, no one was listening any more. Without the air of menace that hung over the G20 in 2009, Gordon's broader plans failed to impress themselves on the others. He tries to convince himself that the cause is not lost and that what was achieved at the depths of the crisis still remains as 'a model, a way of working together, that could shape global financial co-operation to prevent and deal with crises in the future'. But you feel he knows that what he achieved was probably the limit of what he could have achieved. He ends his account of these tumultuous events with a defiant echo of what he said when he quoted his old school motto outside Number Ten on his first day as prime minister: 'I had done my best.'

The other great crisis that suited Brown's political temperament was the one that hit long after he had quit Downing Street. He played a vital role in preventing the break-up of the UK in 2014, when his tireless and passionate interventions in the Scottish independence referendum campaign helped shore up support for the Union among wavering Scots. His arguments were built on the idea that Scottish patriotism could be accommodated within the Union, but only if it was respected as distinctively Scottish. Uniquely among leading pro-Union politicians, Brown saw that the Scots should not be told what they ought to do. Instead of being told, they needed to be heard. He pushed hard for Westminster politicians to make far bigger concessions to Scottish wishes to have more control over their own affairs. His speeches worked not because he had the best arguments but because he understood the frustrations of his audience. He was as aggrieved by the cack-handedness of the Better Together campaign as they were. Brown repeatedly warned Cameron and Osborne that Project Fear wouldn't work, and that only Project Listen (in the form of a promise to devolve more powers, finally made in the week before the vote) would salvage the situation. He was right. The proof came two years later, when Cameron and Osborne persisted with Project Fear right up to the bitter end of the Brexit campaign, and lost it.

Brown's sense of achievement comes across in a vivid account of the speech he gave in Maryhill twenty-four hours before the final vote in the Scottish referendum. It was probably the best speech of his life, even though – or perhaps precisely because – he had to cut his usual forty-five-minute stump address down to thirteen minutes to fit a very tight schedule. Moments before he was due to go on, someone whispered in his ear: 'Your right shoe is covered in mud.' Brown managed to delay his entrance just long enough to allow a frantic aide to claw off the mud with a paper towel, while the comedian Eddie Izzard introduced him from the stage. That uncharacteristically jaunty little anecdote, with its combination of gentle name-dropping and clumsy high jinks, shows how much Brown still treasures the memory. The speech ended with his plea to the crowd: 'Tell them this is our Scotland.' He was speaking for them, not to them, and both he and they relished this fact.

What makes it more poignant is that it comes towards the end of a political life dominated by memories of speeches that were far less successful. Brown normally put far more into his speeches than he ever got back. It was not for want of trying. When describing his typical day as PM, he says one reason he needed to be at his desk so early that morning was because 'a speech for me was usually the culmination of a hundred drafts, constantly rewritten, updated and refined.' A hundred? If that's even half true, it goes beyond diligence and comes close to OCD. It is painful to think of him endlessly trying to find the form of words that would nail the case he was trying to make, and never quite getting there. This quixotic attachment to the pursuit of the decisive argument cost him dear.

He knows it. When John Smith died in 1994, he spent too long working on his obituary in the hours after the death was announced ('I wanted to do his life and achievements justice'), allowing Blair to steal a vital march on him in the more impor-tant business of politicking for the succession. Brown then compounded the mistake two days after Smith was buried.

I made my speech in honour of him at the Welsh Labour conference in Swansea in which I set out a vision of a party awash with ideas, vibrant with dynamism and purpose, that would reform the welfare state and appeal beyond our heartlands. It did not make the impact with the media that I had hoped. I had an agreement with Tony that we would not attack each other's speeches, but a briefing went around that I had made my appeal to what an unidentified briefer termed – without a hint of irony – 'forces of darkness' within the party.

As he admits when discussing another speech that really did make a difference: 'Not all speeches matter.' The irony here, though, is that the speech in question was not one of his own. It was given by John Prescott a year before Smith's death, in defence of the Labour leader's fraught attempt to get One Member, One Vote past the trades unions at the Labour Conference. Prescott's approach to oratory was the opposite of Brown's – if he wrote more than one draft, never mind one hundred, it would be a surprise. The speech worked for the same reason Brown's Scotland speeches worked: it wasn't the preparation, or the argument, or the diligence, but the sense of identity. Prescott won over his audience despite (or more likely because of) all the bluster and brinkmanship. He convinced them he wasn't speaking to them, never mind at them. He was speaking with them.

Brown has also been a prolific writer, though whether his publications made any more difference than his speeches is an open question. Whenever his political career hits a slow patch, Brown's impulse seems to have been to churn out another volume of well-intentioned, earnest prose. *Courage* (2007), *Britain's Everyday Heroes* (2007), *The Change We Choose* (2010), *Beyond the Crash* (2010) – for a busy prime minister, that's a lot of book-writing. Even Gladstone and Disraeli would be impressed by the industry, though presumably a little embarrassed by the quality. The persistent impression Brown gives is of a man who doesn't know when to stop digging with his pen, looking for gold.

||||
||||

Is Brown's tale ultimately a tragic one, as is sometimes supposed? Was he undone by some fatal flaw? I don't think so. His story is a political one. Like many dominant politicians, he had the strength of his weaknesses and the weaknesses of his strengths. Though it is said that all political lives end in failure, that's not really true either. They end in politics. Brown's paranoia, which served him so well in the depths of the financial crisis, let him down over Iraq. He writes that he should have been more suspicious of the intelligence the British government was being fed by the Americans. But he couldn't afford to be. He was, in 2002, already fighting Blair on a number of fronts – 'the euro, the NHS, tuition fees' are the ones he lists – and 'rightly or wrongly, I was anxious to avoid a fourth area of dispute, particularly one that was not my departmental responsibility'. So he shirked it, unlike the foreign secretary, Robin Cook, who showed in his resignation speech what could be known about what was not known at the time. Brown now feels that 'we were all misled on the existence of WMDs'. In fact, he is convinced that the Bush administration duped them: 'Somewhere in the American system the truth about Iraq's lack of weapons was known.' But being paranoid after the event is no good to anyone.

Brown also misjudged the coalition negotiations in 2010. Though he lost the election, he thought the Lib Dems were far closer to Labour on most policy questions than they were to the Tories. He genuinely believed it ought to have been possible to put together a stop-the-Tories coalition, given that a significant majority of the electorate had voted for what he saw as parties of the centre-left. So if Nick Clegg wasn't willing to deal with him, it must have been because he was a secret Tory all along. He wasn't; he was just a realist, and after three years of Brown he knew the country needed a change. Brown warned him that if he got into bed with Cameron he would regret it. 'The Tories will destroy you, I said. And they will pull us all apart on Europe.' Brown was right about that. In politics it is possible to be right and wrong at the same time.

Brown's telling of his life story captures what made him such a distinctive politician. Reading it is an authentic experience, full of contradictions. Some of the writing is utterly pedestrian, but some of it is compelling, and more. I was moved to tears by Brown's account of the death of his baby daughter, Jennifer, at one week old.

> She was baptised on the Sunday in her cot in the Royal Infirmary ward [...] I held Jennifer in my arms – her beautiful face still unaffected, untouched by the scale of the tragedy that had befallen her. Sarah and I took our vows as parents to do everything to bring her up 'in the nurture and admonition of the Lord'. The baptism was for us not just a comfort or a ritual: it was a recognition that every single life, even the shortest one, had a purpose and every person is irreplaceable. The Saturday, Sunday and Monday were essentially a vigil. We spent Jennifer's last nights taking it in turns to be at her bedside and sleeping next door in a room set aside for parents of critically ill children. There was nursing help to ensure Jennifer had no pain or suffering. We were with her all Monday afternoon as her life ebbed away. We held her in our arms as she died at 5 p.m.

Then, on the same page, he writes of his gratitude to the tabloid editors Paul Dacre of the *Daily Mail* and Piers Morgan of the *Daily Mirror* for their help in sparing them from the intrusions of the press during that dreadful time. 'We remain grateful to this day.' Oh, that band of brothers.

6

THE ONES WHO GOT AWAY

NOWADAYS, ALONG WITH a good lawyer, an agent and a PR representative, celebrity miscreants need an enabler: the person who indulged them in their vices and so can be blamed for failing to get them to stop. Who enabled Tiger Woods? Who enabled Harvey Weinstein? Who enabled Kevin Spacey? Such questions, like 'Who lost China?', seem to demand an answer, even though the real answer is that these people, like China, are responsible for their own fate. Enablers to the rich and famous usually fall into the uncertain category that lies somewhere between employee and friend, which is what makes it so hard for them to call time on their boss/buddy's misbehaviour. They are the people who go to the parties, make sure the girls/boys and the drugs find their way to the right table, then help to clear up the mess in the morning. But enablers are also useful when the mess comes to light, because they can be cast as the villains of the piece, the ones who allowed the whole thing to spin out of control. How can anyone be expected to get a handle on his or her problems when surrounded by lickspittles like these? By dumping on the enabler, the celebrity can be recast in the more comfortable role of victim.

Enablers are less useful, however, when they decide to tell their side of the story – indeed, then they become positively terrifying. These aren't just the people who know where the bodies are buried. They're the ones who drove you to the site, handed over the spade and whistled to keep your spirits up while you were digging. Usually that kind of complicity should be enough to guarantee silence. But it also means that once someone decides to spill the beans, it's because they've decided there is nothing left to lose. This certainly appears to be the case with Andrew Young, whose stomach-churning, jaw-dropping account of his time spent working for, befriending and then covering up on behalf of the Democratic politician and presidential hopeful John Edwards takes the genre of enabler's revenge to a whole new level. 'Covering up' doesn't really do justice to Young's role, which by the end included going on the run with Edwards's mistress Rielle Hunter and their love child (with Young's own wife and three children in tow), having allowed Edwards to tell the press that he – Young – was the father of Hunter's baby. How does anyone get into the position of accepting paternity of another man's child in order to allow him to continue running for president? Young sets out to explain, and it does not make for pretty reading.

What is clear from the start is that this is a love story. The real romance is not the one between Edwards and the extremely peculiar Hunter, a self-described 'truth seeker' and 'old soul' who needs to call her psychic guru back in California before she can decide whether to have Russian dressing with her Reuben sandwich. The love is between Young and Edwards, even though from the start it is distressingly one-way. Young was, on his own account, a pretty easy catch. He first sees Edwards at a lawyers' convention in Myrtle Beach, and is blown away by his fresh-faced looks, his ready charisma and his palpable sincerity. The deal is sealed when Young catches sight of Edwards opening the door of his beaten-up Buick and picking up the old Diet Coke can that falls out to dispose of it in the trash. Not only is this a rich man who drives an ordinary car, but it is a rich man who deals with his own rubbish rather than leaving it for others to take care of! By the time Young discovers that Edwards has got BMWs and Lexus coupés stashed away at home, and that he brings out the Buick only when he needs to burnish his everyman image, it is too late – he has been sucked in.

The Edwards whom Young went to work for was a relative newcomer to politics, having made his fortune as a trial lawyer specialising in medical malpractice suits. The event that changed Edwards's life was the death of his teenage son Wade in a road accident in 1996. His response to this tragedy was to spend a chunk of his personal fortune getting himself elected to the US Senate for his home state of North Carolina, though not before he had enhanced that fortune by deploying the story of his son's death during his closing remarks in a case against a swimming-pool company whose suction cleaner had disembowelled a young girl, helping him to secure a $25 million verdict for his clients. Young tells us that Edwards decided on a political career when he watched the movie *The American President*, which stars Michael Douglas as a widowed president who falls in love with a lobbyist. Apparently the film helped Edwards to imagine 'a life of purpose following a great personal loss'. (Incidentally, it also means that two of the three main Democrat contenders for the presidency in 2008 were partly the creation of Aaron Sorkin, screenwriter of *The American President* and originator of *The West Wing*, which more or less mapped out Obama's run for the presidency before it happened; in that sense, only Hillary Clinton was 'real'.) The response of Edwards's formidable wife, Elizabeth, to the loss of Wade was to abandon her own success-ful legal career in order to undergo fertility treatment at the age of forty-eight, after which she gave birth to two more children. She also devoted herself to furthering her husband's ambitions to move as quickly as he could from the Senate to the White House. Political ambition, like marriage, is a deeply mysterious thing when seen from the outside.

Bereavement is the motor that propels this story: the Edwardses are two driven, restless people who, unhinged by grief, become in their different ways even more driven and even more restless. It also provides some gruesomely comic moments along the way. In 2004 Edwards put up a decent showing in the Democratic presidential primaries, which persuaded the successful candidate, John Kerry, to consider him as his vice-presidential running mate. The two men, who did not know each other well, arranged a meeting in Washington to see how they might get along. The meeting was not a success. Edwards, in order to establish some intimacy, told Kerry he wanted to share a story with him that no one else knew. He then proceeded to tell him that, when he was brought to identify his son's body, he climbed on the mortuary slab in order to embrace him one last time. Kerry was stunned, not so much by the inappropriateness of the tale as by the fact that Edwards had told him the same story on one of the few occasions they had met previously. Edwards's own response to this encounter, which also saw Elizabeth get together with Teresa Heinz Kerry for the first time, was to tell Young that both Kerrys were 'complete assholes'. Part of the problem was that they had too much money for Edwards's liking: 'Andrew, I'm rich, but they are ludicrously rich. How can he possibly be the leader of the Democratic Party?'

Edwards, whose political career was built on his supposed empathy with the common man, turns out to be obsessed with the distinction between two classes in American society: the people who are what he calls 'rich like me' and the people whom he refers to as 'really, really rich'. (As far as one can tell, it's the difference between having a net worth in eight figures and one in nine or ten.) Despite all this, Kerry picked Edwards, and despite the spectacular lack of personal chemistry between them, the two men held it together long enough to come tantalisingly close to victory. Unsurprisingly, both Edwardses blamed both Kerrys for the ultimate failure to unseat George W. Bush. They thought Kerry ran a lacklustre campaign, that Teresa was a drag from the start and that only jealousy could explain the reluctance to give John, with all his natural charms, a more prominent role. Next time, the Edwardses were deter- mined that they would be in charge.

||||
||||

Everything changes again for John and Elizabeth Edwards on the night in November 2004 when they discover that the American people (or rather a couple of hundred thousand of them in Ohio) have granted Bush/Cheney four more years. However, it is not the little death of electoral defeat that marks the shift. It is instead thoughts of another death, this time of a death foretold. Elizabeth learns at just the moment the election results are coming in that she has cancer, and the prog- nosis is not good. By this point Young is working for the family in North Carolina as a kind of glorified bagman, running errands, raising political funds, organising the daily schedule (Edwards has quit the Senate, so has no political staff in Wash- ington to arrange how he spends his time). Young is the person Elizabeth calls when she needs someone to summon plumbers in a domestic emergency or drive former staffers to retrain- ing programmes or get hold of a special birthday gift for one of her kids. This last task produces one of the major fallings- out of Young's period in her service, when his own assistant invokes the Edwards name to jump the queue at Walmart in an attempt to get hold of a Sony PlayStation 3. This does not look good when Walmart publicises it the next day, since John Edwards was the leader of a campaign protesting against Walmart's failure to offer healthcare coverage to its workers and its refusal to allow them to unionise. The press and late- night talk shows have a field day. So does Elizabeth Edwards, who sends Young a series of increasingly abusive emails. One of these ends: 'This is what can happen when we ask for special treatment. We cannot ask for special treatment. Ever.' If this is the Edwards family motto, it should perhaps come with the rider that what they do instead is wait for special treatment to be offered without their having to ask for it.

Young gets to witness up close Elizabeth's increasingly erratic and vindictive behaviour as her illness takes its toll. Far from asking her husband to scale back his political ambitions, she pushes him on, if anything even more determined than he is to ensure he comes out on top in 2008. But her political judgement is gone. The big favour she does ask of John is that he build her a dream mansion in Chapel Hill, complete with indoor swimming-pool and matching tree houses for the children, each measuring more than 1,000 square feet. This is his 'cancer gift' to her, but when it gets built, not only is it a significant drain on the family finances (remember, the Edwardses are only rich, not really, really rich), but it also does huge damage to his man-of-the-people credentials when aerial shots of the 100-acre estate appear online.

Meanwhile, it seems that John's cancer gift to himself was to take a mistress. Young would have us believe that this came as something of a shock to his loyal staff, who had often assumed that their boss was asexual. Again, Young might have been more assiduous in following up earlier clues: he admits that it was part of his job to gather up and dispose of the notes that eager young women would try to palm on to the senator during campaign visits, and that every now and again Edwards would grab one of these and slip it into his jacket pocket. Anyway, some time early in 2006 Rielle Hunter appears as part of the entourage, ostensibly in the role of film-maker recording a video diary of Edwards's campaigning trips. Soon she is accompanying him on overseas missions, hanging out in his hotel room and eventually sleeping with him in the marital bed on the nights Elizabeth is away. Young's time is increasingly taken up with ensuring that Hunter and Edwards can maintain contact without Elizabeth finding out. He isn't happy about this – and his long-suffering wife, Cheri, is even less so – but he sees it as part of the job. After all, his personal mission statement to himself when he began working for Edwards was to 'set a new standard for body men', meeting all his boss's personal needs and asking no questions. What else was he supposed to do?

Hunter turns out to be a difficult woman to please. She pesters Young constantly, demanding to know why Edwards can't spend more time with her and complaining whenever she can't get through to him on the phone. In an earlier incarnation, when she had been called Lisa Druck, Hunter had briefly dated Jay McInerney, and is reputed to have inspired the character of the horrible, cocaine-addled sex fiend Alison Poole, who appears in several of McInerney's novels. When Young eventually finds a videotape of Hunter and Edwards having sex and considers whether he can use it to gain some leverage over them, he wonders whether his story and theirs are in danger of turning into a John Grisham thriller, with all the potential for violence that that involves. But really Hunter's tale belongs to a darker, more Faulknerian strain of fiction. When she was a teenager, her father, James Druck, was implicated in a notorious scam that involved killing horses in order to claim on the insurance; he ended his daughter's promising equestrian career by paying someone to electrocute her prize pony. After that, she seems to have had, as they say, daddy issues.

The great unravelling begins on the night that Elizabeth Edwards first sets eyes on Rielle preening herself at a campaign event and instantly guesses that this woman is sleeping with her husband. When she confronts John, she manages to extract what might at best be called a part confession. Later, Young discovers 'that the senator had told Elizabeth that although he had indulged in a "one-night" fling with Rielle, in recent weeks she had become my [i.e., Young's] mistress!' Showing commendable restraint, this is the only exclamation mark that Young uses throughout his narrative – if nothing else, he is a man who knows how to punctuate. Unsurprisingly, Elizabeth turns on Young, showering him with vicious emails and encouraging the rest of her husband's staff to disown him. She also starts trawling obsessively through the videos that Hunter has made of her husband on the road, looking for clues. But if anything, Edwards's outrageous slander serves to bring him and his body man closer together. Young takes it as a sign of how dependent his boss has become on him that he needs him to fulfil the role of fall guy. He is now the person standing between Edwards's presidential ambitions and ruin. So when Rielle reveals she is pregnant, it is naturally Young to whom Edwards turns to make the necessary arrangements, including finding her somewhere to live away from journalistic prying eyes. This turns out to mean that Hunter has to move in with Young and his family, and all of them have to move out of his own home and into a series of luxurious safe houses paid for from somewhere in the dark recesses of the Edwards political operation. Throughout it all Young's wife remains remarkably stoical, while never believing for a moment that it'll do any good. She's right, of course. Eventually the *National Enquirer* gets photographic proof that the woman they believe to be John Edwards's mistress is with child. Faced with this calamity, Edwards somehow persuades Young to put his name to the following press release:

> As confirmed by Ms Hunter, Andrew Young is the father of her unborn child. Senator Edwards knew nothing about the relationship between these former co-workers, which began when they worked together in 2006. As a private citizen who no longer works for the campaign, Mr Young asks that the media respect his privacy while he works to make amends with his family.

The response of the *Enquirer* to this unambiguous statement of fact is the obvious one: yeah, right. They publish the John Edwards Love Child Scandal! story anyway, with the following disclaimer stuck on the end:

And in a bizarre twist, Young – a 41-year-old married man with young children – now claims he is the father of Rielle's baby! But others are skeptical, wondering if Young's paternity claim is a cover-up to protect Edwards.

When the *Enquirer* is on the side of scepticism, you know you are in deep trouble.

||||

How on earth did it come to this? Young was trying to keep his boss in the presidential race, and incredibly, for a time, he succeeded. The *Enquirer* story ran in late December 2007, just days before the Iowa primary for the Democratic nomination. Though the online world exploded with speculation about what Edwards was up to, the mainstream media kept its distance from the story, nervous of getting sucked into such murky waters when the primary season was upon them. In Iowa, Edwards managed to come a creditable second to Obama, squeezing Hillary Clinton into third place. Unfortunately, he had gambled everything on winning Iowa, and once it was clear that this was now the Barack'n'Hillary show, he got crushed in New Hampshire. Still, he hung on in the race, hoping to parlay his small number of delegates into influence at the convention and possibly a big job afterwards. In late February, Hunter had her baby, but the press continued to keep its silence, and Edwards continued to campaign as the honest broker for an increasingly divided and fractious Democratic Party. It was only in June, when the *Enquirer* snatched some photos of Edwards visiting Hunter and the baby at a hotel in Los Angeles, that the truth started to come out. Edwards gave a disastrously misjudged 'confessional' interview to ABC, in which he admitted having made a 'mistake' but still professed undying devotion to Elizabeth. ('I'm in love with one woman. I've been in love with one woman for thirty-one years. She is the finest human being I have ever known,' and so, nauseatingly, on.) This time the response of almost everyone was: yeah, right (apart from Bill Clinton, who apparently rang Edwards up to ask him, 'How'd you get caught?'). In due course, the only woman John Edwards has ever been in love with formally separated from him when a paternity test confirmed he was the father of Hunter's child. Elizabeth Edwards died of cancer at the end of 2010, unreconciled to her husband. He also became permanently estranged from his one-time friend and employee Andrew Young.

Young's motivations throughout this extraordinary tale are simultaneously transparent and deeply mysterious. He loved being around Edwards for the proximity it gave him to money, power and celebrity. He also seemed to share his boss's belief that he was destined for ever greater things. When family and friends press Young on why he is willing to give so much time and energy to serving this man, his answer from back in 2004 is the mantra: 'Sixteen years in the White House!' It's a seductive idea: Edwards serves as Kerry's VP, then gets the nomination as if by right, and takes his own turn at the top, with Young following in his wake. But it's also pure fantasy, even before Edwards has started to stray. No American politician of any stripe has ever managed sixteen years in the White House – it requires too many contingencies to fall into place. Why would John Edwards, his obvious gifts (folksy charm, lawyerly ruthlessness, full head of hair) notwithstanding, be the first? Nevertheless, after the defeat of Kerry/Edwards in 2004, Edwards convinces himself, and many of those around him, that he is the obvious choice for 2008, in what will be the most winnable election for a Democratic candidate for many years. He positioned himself to the left of Hillary Clinton (disastrously, he more or less ignored the challenge posed by Obama until it was too late) and worked hard to win support among labour organisations and blue-collar Americans worried about their jobs and their health insurance (or lack of it). He is the man who is going to deliver not just the White House for the Democratic Party but also the first serious legislative programme to tackle poverty and inequality in the US for more than a generation. He will be the LBJ of the early twenty-first century. Whenever Young complains about the increasingly miserable and undignified demands that Edwards is placing on him as he pursues this dream, the standard response he gets is: 'This is bigger than any of us.'

But there are other forces at work. Young hints at his own chequered past, in which alcohol often played a part. He hits a low when, after a fight with his wife, he gets arrested for drink-driving and loses his licence. Terrified of what this will mean when the Edwardses find out (apart from anything else, he knows he is much less useful if he can't ferry them around), he is amazed and relieved by his employer's deeply empathetic response: 'We've all done something like this, Andrew. I have. I know you feel like the lowest person on earth right now, but I love you. You are like a brother to me.' What this also means, however, is that Young is now deeply in his debt, and they both know it. But the real glue that keeps Young in place is the American healthcare system, a subject on which Edwards had made himself an expert and the reform of which formed the centrepiece of his bid for the presidency.

Two of Young's three children experience serious medical problems in the first year of their lives that require expensive treatment. On the rare occasions Young considers breaking his ties with the Edwardses and starting afresh, the first thing that comes to mind is that they are paying not only his wages but his family's health insurance as well. And, since his children have pre-existing conditions, it always gives him pause. Young's story is, among many other things, a truly chilling portrayal of the way healthcare worked in the US pre-Obamacare. The treatment the Youngs' second child gets, even with insurance, is haphazard at best, with diagnostic failures and inadequate nursing. When they complain, someone from the hospital's

Risk Management Office is sent to calm them down. By the time their third child develops similar problems, they have learned enough about the importance of personal contacts to trade on the Edwards name to get the best treatment available. Meanwhile, when Rielle Hunter arrives at a hospital in California to give birth to John Edwards's child, it turns out she has no insurance at all. Young has to front up $5,000 on his own credit card just to get her admitted. Finally, always hovering somewhere in the background at the bleaker moments of the story, is Elizabeth Edwards's state of health.

It is hard to escape the conclusion that it is the prospect of his wife dying that drives John Edwards to behave in the way he does. Sometimes this is made explicit and Edwards exploits the fact of his wife's disease to put off difficult decisions, as when Young pleads with him to tell her the truth about the paternity of Hunter's baby, and he responds: 'I can't let her die knowing this.' At other points, however, the unspoken thought arises that Edwards's extraordinarily reckless behaviour only makes sense if he believes that becoming a widower will relieve him of its potentially most dangerous consequences (exposure and ruin). When he asks Young (who in comparison with Edwards is really, really poor) to lend money to Hunter, he reassures him that everything would be repaid 'when a wealthy benefactor was recruited to cover these costs or when Mrs Edwards died'. He doesn't say which he expects sooner. But it is Young himself who finally says the unsayable, albeit only in the retrospective form of his memoir. Thinking through his options during the days between the Iowa and New Hampshire primaries of 2008, he comes to this conclusion:

> If [Edwards] got the nomination and Mrs Edwards survived, we would be hard-pressed to find a way out of our arrangement with Rielle before November. If he didn't win the nomination but wanted to pursue either the vice-presidential slot or a place in some future Democratic

administration, we'd be in the same predicament. Barring
a sudden surge of honesty, the only way we were going
to get out of our commitment would be if Mrs Edwards
died. And we still loved her too much to hope for this
terrible outcome.

By 'we', he means himself and Cheri. He does not presume to
speak for the senator.

It is hardly surprising that no one emerges well out of this
story. Yet one of the things it leaves you wondering about is
the extent of Edwards's qualities as a politician. Certainly he
comes across as a narcissist, a hypocrite and someone capable
of extraordinary insensitivity. His personal life isn't fit for
public consumption. (Then again, whose is?) But one is also left
with considerable admiration for his ability to hold together a
presidential campaign in the face of the mounting chaos of his
private affairs, and he often stays remarkably calm under pressure. At times his ability to compartmentalise seems to border
on genius. He makes the phone call in which he persuades
Young to claim paternity of Hunter's child from Des Moines,
where he is just a couple of hours away from taking part in a
crucial debate against his Democratic rivals. As Young recalls:
'The senator talked as if he had all the time in the world [...]
His demeanour made me think that he possessed at least one
presidential quality: the ability to stay calm in a crisis.' Then,
with only the fig leaf of Young's risible statement to the press
to provide cover, he presses on for another six months, persuading the world that he is a candidate to be taken seriously.
Hillary and Obama remained in desperate competition for his
endorsement, until he finally bestowed it on Obama in May
2008.

Before she died, Elizabeth Edwards threatened to sue
Young, not for libel but for 'alienation of affection', on the
grounds that his role in covering up her husband's affair was in
part responsible for the failure of their marriage. The enabler's

revenge made her determined to get her revenge on the enabler. But if Elizabeth wanted to find someone to blame for concealing the truth about her husband's failings, she should probably have focused her attention on the mainstream media, which when presented with all the evidence they needed by the *National Enquirer*, decided to turn their noses up at it. Calling what Young did a cover-up is a bit much given that it was all so easy to see through, for anyone who chose to look.

‖‖

The mismatch between the public poise and private chaos involved in running for high office, and the reluctance of the press to probe that gap, was a wider theme of the extraordinary 2008 presidential campaign. It wasn't just Edwards. In fact, it may be that one of the reasons Edwards's misdemeanours didn't the get attention they deserved is that they didn't really stand out from everything else that was happening. In John Heilemann and Mark Halperin's *Race of a Lifetime*, which tells the story of 2008 from inside the camp of all the leading candidates, the Edwards fiasco gets relatively short shrift. Apart from brevity, the main difference from Young's account is that their sources are other Edwards aides, who take the opportunity to dump all over Young. Young's 'devotion to his boss was comically servile,' they write. One of Edwards's staffers liked to joke, 'If John asked Andrew to wipe his ass, he would say, "What kind of toilet paper?"' But the travails of the Edwardses appear simply as an extreme version of what's going on inside many of the other campaigns, with fears of bimbo eruptions, psychic trauma, financial ruin and family breakdown looming large for all of them. Or rather, for all of them bar one. Barack Obama emerges as different from the rest. He is portrayed as calm, faithful and emotionally secure. Obama, we are told, 'rejected the notion that running for president was a task suited only to the borderline mentally ill'. Heilemann and

Halperin do everything they can to back up the double implication of this statement: first, by showing how Obama kept his
head when all around him were losing theirs; and second, by
showing his rivals losing theirs in ways you would not believe.

The implicit justification for this kind of tell-all account
is that the truth about the people running for president can
only be seen behind the scenes, where the craziness is on full
display. Exhibit one is Hillary Clinton on the night that she
gets beaten by Obama and Edwards into third place in Iowa.
Having been reluctantly persuaded by her staff to commit
huge amounts of time and resources to a contest she had her
own doubts about winning, she explodes with rage and resent-
ment when the results come in. Red-faced and barely coherent,
she lashes out at those around her, and can barely bring herself
to be civil to Obama when she calls to congratulate him.
'Watching her bitter and befuddled reaction, her staggering
lack of calm or command, one of her senior-most lieutenants
thought for the first time, *This woman shouldn't be president.*'
This is one of Heilemann and Halperin's recurring motifs: the
moment when loyal staffers are confronted with the apparent unsuitability of their candidates for the highest office. It
happens with John McCain, when he explodes with rage at
his wife or blusters incoherently at an economic briefing; with
Edwards, of course, as he makes a fool of himself over Hunter;
and above all, with McCain's running mate, Sarah Palin, who
seems to leave her staff in a semi-permanent state of despair at
her unpreparedness for it all. By contrast, Obama is presented
as consistently confounding the expectations of his staff by
being better than they dared hope. When a deeply anxious
David Axelrod, Obama's chief strategist, is emailed a copy of
Obama's speech on race, designed to defuse the rapidly escal-
ating row about the behaviour of his pastor, the Rev. Wright,
he fires back a one-line response: 'This is why you should be
president.' Another of his staffers, Anita Dunn, recalls thinking
at the same time: 'This is a guy I want in a foxhole with me.'

The one respect in which Obama comes across as comparable to his rivals is in his frustration with the mainstream media. What bothers him is not so much their coverage of his own campaign (how could he be bothered, given how besotted with him most journalists were?) as their failure to expose what he knows about the bad behaviour going on elsewhere. Why didn't they nail Hillary for her covert racism, and her husband for his deliberate misrepresentations of the Obama message? Here is one of the deep puzzles of electoral politics: all the candidates spend a considerable chunk of their time manipulating the media, and much of the rest of their time complaining about the media's failure to see through the obvious obfuscations of their opponents. There is some serious cognitive dissonance going on here: the politicians are both terrified and contemptuous of the newspapers at the same time. So the Hillary camp consume countless hours in fretful anticipation of a *New York Times* exposé of her husband's post-White House infidelities; but when it comes, it is such a damp squib that they brush it off with barely a second thought. The same happens to the McCain campaign, where staffers are endlessly worrying that the *Times* is going to destroy their candidate with tales of an inappropriate relationship during his time in the Senate, but end up closing down the story once it appears by the simple device of getting McCain to deny it. But none of this stops McCain and Clinton raging against the same newspaper for its failure to pursue all the murky links and dodgy deals that they feel certain loom large in Obama's Chicago past. In fact, the exaggerated fear they all have of scandalous newspaper headlines is one of the things that helps to keep the press servile – no story ever quite matches the apocalyptic expectations that precede it, which makes any story that actually gets published much easier to discount because it failed to deliver the knock-out blow.

Heilemann and Halperin would like us to think that theirs is the story we weren't allowed to see at the time it was happening because the mainstream media wouldn't have dared report it and the candidates wouldn't have let them. The clear implication is that the American voting public can be left reassured by the choice they eventually made: apart from Obama, would you want any of these deeply damaged individuals to have wound up in the White House? That may have been how it looked back in 2008. After the 2016 election we know there was far worse to come. But there is another way to look at it. As with Edwards, it is possible to lament the bad behaviour yet to remain impressed by the way these deeply damaged individuals managed to hold their campaigns together and present a reasonable face to the public, despite all the madness going on behind the scenes. The fact that Hillary completely lost her cool after coming third to Obama in Iowa doesn't mean she wasn't qualified to be president; certainly it doesn't outweigh the qualifications she showed by pulling herself together, getting back out there and turning the tables on him in New Hampshire five days later. Resilience, competitiveness and sheer bloody-mindedness are political strengths, as much as coolness, detachment and personal equilibrium. And even those candidates whose private failings would give anyone pause at seeing their hand on the nuclear trigger still emerge as having a quality that always counts for something in politics: the ability to stick it out regardless.

The person who comes out from the 2008 campaign worst in this sense, but also best, is Sarah Palin. She was terrifyingly out of her depth, and much of the blame for this lies with John McCain, who chose her as his running mate only at the very last moment, having been dissuaded from going with his first preference, Joe Lieberman. McCain had been attracted to Lieberman (Al Gore's running mate in 2000, but by then sitting as an independent in the Senate, having been disowned by his party for his full-throated support of the Iraq War), because such an unlikely choice seemed to fit with his self-projection as a maverick. When it finally dawned on him that the Republican Party wouldn't stand for it, he decided to double down on his maverick credentials by gambling on the woman from Alaska, who looked great on paper but about whom he knew next to nothing. This late switch left McCain's staff less than a week to vet Palin and to prep her for the mind-blowing shift from Alaskan state politics to being one of the most famous people in the world. No one knew how she would cope. On the night of her speech to the nominating convention, McCain was waiting anxiously backstage, barely able to watch as Palin embarked on her first major public appearance. His temporary euphoria shows that he was as clueless as everyone else about what to expect. 'McCain went from pacing fretfully to murmuring, "She's really good," to enthusing, "She's incredible," to grabbing [one of his aides] and exulting, "Oh, my God, great job, she did a great job!"' Indeed she did – if not the best speech of the entire campaign, it was certainly the funniest, and Obama never delivered a line as good as her 'I guess a small-town mayor is sort of like a community organiser, except that you have actual responsibilities.'

After that dazzling debut, however, things started to go very badly wrong. Palin became first distracted, then sullen, then completely withdrawn as the step up to a national campaign started to overwhelm her. Though initially enthusiastic, she soon began to resent the endless tutoring sessions with McCain staffers who were desperately trying to plug the yawning gaps in her knowledge of world affairs. She missed her family, including her newborn son Trig, and may have been suffering from post-natal depression (unless you believe the conspiracy theorists who still insist the baby is not hers but her daughter's – somewhat ironic for a campaign when people were also willing to believe that Edwards's daughter was not his but his aide's). By the time the McCain team took Palin into seclusion to prepare for her one and only vice-presidential debate with Joe Biden (a man she was unable to stop herself calling 'Senator O'Biden'), it was clear that she was sick, and they were terrified:

Never before had Palin's team seen her so profoundly out of sorts for such a sustained period. She wasn't eating (a few small bites of steak a day, no more). She wasn't drinking (maybe half a can of Diet Dr Pepper, no water, ever). She wasn't sleeping (not much more than a couple of hours a night, max). The index cards were piling up by the hundreds, but Palin wasn't absorbing the material written on them. When her aides tried to quiz her, she would routinely shut down – chin on her chest, arms folded, eyes cast to the floor, speechless and motionless, lost in what those around her described as a kind of cata-tonic stupor.

This is clearly a person in the middle of a major depressive episode. It was around this time that Palin gave her notorious interview with Katie Couric, in which she did indeed appear catatonic, as we now know that she was. And yet, somehow, she kept going, and in the end she pulled through. She not only survived her debate with Biden (having solved the problem of her inability to remember his name by saying at the outset, 'Hey, can I call you Joe?'), she battled him to a draw, and then went on to rally the Republican faithful in a series of barn-storming performances around the country. Clearly, in drawing back the curtain to reveal the psychological disorder behind the scenes, Heilemann and Halperin want us to recoil in horror, or at the very least to wince with pity. But I found myself struck with wonder at the inner resolve of someone who can have a nervous breakdown in the middle of a presidential campaign yet still emerge from it as a significant political figure, someone who barely twelve months later had a large part of the Repub-lican Party in her pocket. Seven years after that she was still going, blazing the trail for Donald Trump as one of the first senior Republicans to endorse him for president. Truly, in this game, what doesn't kill you makes you stronger.

History favours the winners, and so do political tell-alls.

The people who worked with Obama in 2008 never had the same incentive to vent their frustrations as the employees of the other candidates, since the election outcome made all their hard work seem worthwhile (not just with the fact of victory but with power, influence, jobs). For everyone else, Heilemann and Halperin's book offered another version of the enabler's revenge, with the added benefit of anonymity. The people doing the complaining were invariably the ones who spent much of the period in question covering for the bad behaviour that they complain about. Obama unquestionably comes across on this account as the nicest, most reassuring boss, sensible, easy-going and relatively forgiving. The question is why this should matter so much. They were all in it to win it, and in that context Obama is the one whose ambition has done the least to corrode his decency as a human being. But there were glimpses of another Obama in 2008 too: the one who, lest we forget, floundered in debate after debate with Hillary Clinton, her 'mastery of the issues' making him come across as 'vague and weak and windy'.

Obama's confidence in the face of his inadequate grip on policy often looked a lot like arrogance, and his great gifts only really flowered in situations when he could remove himself from the fray. It is no coincidence that the two most significant triumphs of Obama's campaign – his defusing of the Rev. Wright row with his elegant speech on race and his calm handling of the post-Lehman crisis while McCain was flailing around like a lost child – occurred because he felt able to distance himself from events for which he did not feel personally responsible. Obama was good at taking a detached view of other people's failings. It is not clear how good he was at taking a detached view of his own.

Obama unquestionably ran a better campaign than Hillary Clinton. This does not prove that he was bound to be the better president. I have long thought that Hillary would have been the better choice in 2008, just as Obama (who would have been free to run) would have been the best candidate for 2016. Circumstances matter much more than the bare facts about personality. The US story has a British parallel. Though neither Blair nor Brown were ever going to change much as people, how different – and potentially how more successful – the New Labour project might have been if Brown had come first and Blair second. Brown's seriousness of purpose would have suited the early period in power, whereas Blair could have injected some glamour and expansive ideas towards the end. Fate sometimes has a strange way of getting things back to front. Then the first drafts of history conclude that this was the way it was meant to be all along.

Despite the fact that he was obviously unelectable, it is possible to argue that even Edwards had some of the qualities that Obama lacked. By 2008 Edwards had come to know a lot about healthcare reform and other means of tackling inequality, and he had thought seriously about the practical issues involved. He had an understanding of the mindset of the blue-collar workers he would need to win over. He was clear about what he wanted to achieve, and he had a sense of the enemies he would have to make in order to achieve it. He was in some ways fearless, which may have had something to do with the fact that he was also slightly deranged. Obama achieved a lot as president, but there was also a great deal that he left undone. He was no LBJ. At one level Edwards was mad to think he might be. But being mad is part of what means it might have been possible.

It is relatively easy for journalists such as Heilemann and Halperin to hold up the bad behaviour of politicians as a special case and to gawp at the horrors revealed. But politicians are not a special case. Many other people behave badly too, including journalists. In 2017, in the aftermath of the revelations about the conduct of Harvey Weinstein and the subsequent birth of the #MeToo movement, Mark Halperin was accused of serial sexual harassment by more than a dozen women. Some of

these accusations related to his conduct while covering the
presidential elections of 2004 and 2008. He has since lost his
job as a television pundit and had his contract with Heilemann
for a follow-up book telling the inside story of the 2016 election – the craziest election of all – terminated. In 2012 John
Edwards was tried on charges of violating campaign finance
laws. He was acquitted on one count and a mistrial declared
on the other five. Andrew Young took the stand against him.
Inconsistencies in his testimony helped secure his former
boss's acquittal. Edwards has since returned to work as a malpractice lawyer.

What matters is not who people really are. What matters
is what they end up doing with the power they have, large or
small. Even Young, for all his naivety about and complicity in
the miserable tale he has to tell, came to some understanding
of this in the end.

7

BARACK OBAMA

ONE OF THE MINOR DISAPPOINTMENTS about President Obama was that he played golf. It's true that most modern American presidents have liked to play golf – just about everyone from Taft to Trump can be seen with a club in his hand – but Obama was not most presidents. His immediate predecessor, George W. Bush, loved the game but felt he ought to give it up after 9/11, in case it seemed frivolous to be on the golf course when he was sending soldiers into battle. Obama was not so self-denying. He was holidaying on Martha's Vineyard in August 2014 when news came through that the journalist Jim Foley had been beheaded by Isis. The president wrestled with how to respond, reluctant to elevate the outrage but also under mounting pressure to condemn it. In the end Obama offered a forceful denunciation at a hastily arranged press conference at a school on the island, despite his misgivings that he would be delivering Isis just what it wanted: more publicity. But that wasn't the story. His message was overshadowed by his decision to play golf the same afternoon. That's what provoked the outrage.

Obama also played basketball, which made him different from his predecessors. Ben Rhodes, who worked as Obama's deputy national security adviser and his chief foreign policy speechwriter, is one of the very few aides who stayed the course for the entire administration. Rhodes is a 5' 7" balding white man, a worrier and a workaholic who tries to unwind with a drink and a cigarette – a natural fit for golf, in other words. But he was drawn to the basketball player. In his account of his time working in the Obama White House, Rhodes describes the president as a man who 'always moved with ease, like an athlete playing a basketball game at slightly less than a hundred per cent, holding some energy in reserve for the key moments in the fourth quarter'. Obama played on this idea too. After losing seats to the Republicans in the midterm elections of 2014, he rallied his team by declaring: 'My presidency is entering the fourth quarter; interesting stuff happens in the fourth quarter.' One of his staffers was so taken with this line that he had stickers made. 'This elicited some eye-rolling,' Rhodes writes, 'but also a sense that perhaps we were going to spend the last two years of the presidency doing big things, unencumbered by the caution and exhaustion that had crept in.'

As Malcolm Gladwell has pointed out, basketball is the team sport that most depends on the outstanding individual, someone whose outsize talent can carry the weaker players. When LeBron James moves from city to city, the teams he plays for tend to rise and fall with him. Obama was so much more talented than anyone else around – so smart, so eloquent, so cool under pressure – that his team-mates must have hoped he could do the same for them. Golf is different. It's an individualistic game of relentless routine and fine adjustments. The best basketball players win much more often than they lose. Even the very best golfers – Tiger Woods in his prime – lose more often than they win. Golf is a solitary business, and often a lonely one. A basketball team can dominate its opponents and its skilful play will take away from theirs. In golf you are powerless to control what your opponents do. You can only do your best and play the ball where it lies.

Golfer or basketballer? It is striking that, when the calamity arrives that threatens to undo everything he has achieved,

Obama can't decide which way to describe what went wrong. At one point in the dark days that followed Trump's election victory in 2016, he falls back on basketball to explain Hillary Clinton's failure to convert. Rhodes writes:

> He talked about what it took to win the presidency. To win, he told us, you have to have a core reason why you're running, and you need to make it clear to everyone how much you want to win. 'You have to *want* it,' he said, like Michael Jordan demanding the ball in the final moments of a game.

But when provoked, he reaches for a different analogy. On his last overseas trip as president, Obama complains to Rhodes about how he was let down. 'He couldn't believe the election was lost, rattling off the indicators – "Five per cent unemployment. Twenty million covered [by Obamacare]. Gas at two bucks a gallon. *We had it all teed up.*"' This brings to mind an image drawn from another sport: Lucy endlessly lining up the football for Charlie Brown to kick, only to pull it away at the last moment and send him flying. Obama did the opposite of that. He went out of his way to ensure the ball was where it needed to be. All she had to do was swing. *And she whiffed.*

The tug-of-war between the two sides of Obama's sporting personality – the team player and the loner, the dreamer and the realist, the man who thinks anything is still possible and the man who has done his best, then shrugs his shoulders and walks away – is emblematic of his presidency. Rhodes is an instinctive team player and a fervent believer in a better world than the one we currently inhabit. He desperately wants to believe in that side of Obama too. Rhodes went to work for him in the early days of his presidential run in 2007 because he hoped Obama might redeem him from his own original sin, which was to have supported the Iraq War in 2003. Being with Obama gave him the confidence, as he puts it, 'that I was a part of something that was *right* in some intangible way'. He never lost that sense of being on the right side of history, but at many points over the years that followed he came up against Obama's reluctance to embrace the redemptive role in which Rhodes had cast him. Too often Obama was more cautious, more pragmatic, more measured than Rhodes would have liked. Was that just the inevitable deliberation of the person who bore the ultimate responsibility, or was it the essence of the man? 'I wrestled with the constant concern that I was losing myself inside the experience, transformed into a cipher for the needs of this other person who, after all, was a politician, playing the role of US president.' The person, the politician, the president – who was Obama anyway?

⁞⁞⁞

Rhodes could never quite break free from the idea that he and Obama had a special bond, something that transcended their personal circumstances. He persuades himself early on that, notwithstanding their very different backgrounds, he and the president are similar people:

> We both have large groups of friends but maintain a sense of privacy that can lead people to see us as aloof. We're both trying to prove something to our fathers and were nurtured and encouraged by our mothers. We both think of ourselves as outsiders, even when we were in the White House. We're both stubborn – a trait that allows us to take risks that can tip into arrogance. We both act as if we don't care what other people think about us, but we do.

There is something touching about this degree of solipsism. In another life, Rhodes might have made a living as an astrologer. Is there anyone working in Washington politics who couldn't see something of themselves in that description? Yet the one person it doesn't really capture is Obama, who remains unique.

As their working relationship evolves, Rhodes comes to appreciate that Obama does not in fact see things the way he does. How could he, given where he has come from?

> As an African American he had an ingrained scepticism about powerful structural forces that I lacked [...] He had priced in the shortcomings of the world as it is, picking the issues and moments when he could press for the world that ought to be. This illuminated for me his almost monkish, and at times frustrating, discipline in trying to avoid overreach in a roiling world.

Equally, the moments when Obama delivers everything Rhodes could ask are often when the gulf between them is most apparent. One happened in June 2015, after a white supremacist called Dylann Roof walked into a black church in Charleston and shot dead nine members of a Bible study group. The following week Obama spoke at their funeral. After reading from his prepared text, Obama paused.

> It felt as though he'd reached the end of one kind of speech, a particularly good one, but something was not yet fully expressed. Then something changed in his face – a face I had stared at and studied across a thousand meetings, a face I had learned to read so I could understand what he was thinking, or what he wanted me to do. I saw the faintest hint of a smile and a slight shake of the head as he looked down at the lectern, a letting go, a man who looked unburdened. *He's going to sing,* I thought.
> '*Amazing grace, how sweet the sound ...*'

As Obama continues to sing, Rhodes has a kind of epiphany:

I started to feel everything at once – the hurt and anger at the murder of those nine people, another thing that I'd kept pressed down in the constant compartmentalisation of emotions that allowed me to do my job; the stress that comes from doing a job that had steadily swallowed who I thought I was over the last eight years; the more pure motivations, to do something that felt right, buried deep within me.

Rhodes was having an experience that many other people have shared: he wanted Obama to redeem him. Yet he also wanted him to be the politician who delivered lasting change. He had a close enough view of the man himself to know how hard it would be to do both.

For a speechwriter, there was a particular poignancy in realising that being tasked with finding things for Obama to say – with preparing the text – was part of what created the barrier between them. How can Obama be true to himself as Rhodes wants him to be when Rhodes is the person helping make Obama who he is? Sometimes this contrast is so stark it is almost comic, and Rhodes appreciates the irony. When Mandela dies in late 2013, the two men travel together to South Africa as part of a large American entourage for his funeral, at which Obama is due to give an address. It is a richly symbolic moment: the first African-American president paying tribute to Africa's greatest statesman. Rhodes recalls how it felt: 'I was one of those well-meaning white people looking forward to seeing Barack Obama eulogise Nelson Mandela so that I could feel better about the world, only I was the person tasked with writing the eulogy.' In the end, unsatisfied with Rhodes's draft, Obama writes the speech himself. It is much better, but now it is Rhodes's turn to be dissatisfied. He tells the president it is too impersonal: 'You need to put more in here about what Mandela meant to you personally.' Obama has to make his own story part of Mandela's. The president doesn't want to do it – 'I don't want to claim him or put myself in his company' – but in the end he accedes to his speechwriter's advice. 'Over thirty years ago, while still a student, I learned of Nelson Mandela [...] It woke me up to my responsibilities to others and to myself, and it set me on an improbable journey that finds me here today. And while I will always fall short of Madiba's example, he makes me want to be a better man.'

Because Rhodes's job was to write speeches primarily for international audiences, there was always more latitude for these kinds of drama to play out. When not actually going to war, speechmaking is one of the few ways a US president gets to project his vision overseas. In a domestic context, much of Obama's attention during his first term was taken up with technical fixes for the American economy and the messy legislative process of trying to reform the healthcare system. When looking outwards, he could pay more attention to the power of words. 'He turned to speeches as a vehicle to reorient American foreign policy, to communicate a new direction not just to the American people and audiences abroad but to his own government.' Yet because he had his own priorities, his speechwriter often cared more about the impact of these words than the president did. He definitely minded more about preserving the integrity of the brand. When Rhodes organised a trip that took in India, the home of Obama's hero Gandhi, and Indonesia, his home as a boy, the symbolic pay-off should have been a slam dunk for the president. But, coming shortly after his brutal treatment at the hands of the voters in the 2010 midterms, Obama was listless, frustrated and sometimes bored. 'Often,' Rhodes writes, 'I felt as though I cared more about the global progressive icon Barack Obama than Barack Obama did.'

Rhodes is haunted throughout his time in the White House by two earlier catastrophes of US foreign policy, neither of which Obama had any responsibility for, and both of which therefore he might have been able to put right. One is the Iraq

War, which Obama does what he can to get out from under, though it was always going to be too little, too late. The other is the Rwandan genocide. One of Rhodes's heroes is Samantha Power, the person he says 'I most wanted to become when I moved to Washington'. Between 2013 and 2017 Power was the US ambassador to the UN; before that, she lived with 'the permanent tagline "Samantha Power, Pulitzer Prize-winning author of 'A Problem from Hell': America in the Age of Genocide"'.' When the Libya crisis erupts in 2011, Power is on the National Security Council, and at one meeting she passes Rhodes a note saying that if Benghazi is allowed to fall to Gaddafi's forces, 'this was going to be the first mass atrocity that took place on our watch.' Both advisers push Obama hard to sanction military intervention. Obama reluctantly agrees that something must be done.

Two years later, in the summer of 2013, Obama was again under pressure to take military action, this time against Assad in Syria after he had used chemical weapons against his own people in a suburb of Damascus. By now, scarred by the domestic blowback against his Libya policy, Obama is much harder to move. He draws on his own opposition to the Iraq War. '"It is too easy for a president to go to war," he said. "That quote from me in 2007 – I agree with that guy. That's who I am."' Rhodes finds it impossible to argue with this sentiment, but he also finds it difficult to sacrifice his urge to do better than last time. 'It was as if Obama was finally forcing me to let go of a part of who I was – the person who looked at Syria and felt we had to *do something*, who had spent two years searching for hope amid the chaos engulfing the Arab world and the political dysfunction at home.'

Then, a few days later, while preparing for a G20 summit in Russia, Obama goes further. He is sitting with Rhodes in his villa on the grounds of a palace outside St Petersburg, dressed in a grey T-shirt and black sweatpants. An NFL game is on TV in the background. It was like being in 'a neatly appointed condominium you might find alongside a golf course in Arizona'. The discussion turns to growing domestic political opposition to military action in Syria. 'Maybe we never would have done Rwanda,' Obama says. For Rhodes this is the most jarring comment of all. He can't let it go.

> 'You could have done things short of war.'
> 'Like what?'
> 'Like jamming the radio signals they were using to incite people.'
> He waved his hand at me dismissively.
> 'That's wishful thinking. You can't stop people from killing each other like that.'
> He let the thought hang in the air. 'I'm just saying, maybe there's never a time when the American people are going to support this kind of thing.'

Rhodes may have come to Washington wanting to be Samantha Power, but it was asking too much to expect Obama to undergo a similar transformation. He is still 'No Drama' Obama. The guy who managed to get elected in 2008 isn't the guy who is going to get carried away.

IIII

Nevertheless, Rhodes retains a lingering hope that he might get to write the speech that makes all the difference. Being a foreign policy adviser to an American president can feel like getting a ringside seat at the events that shape history. Certainly that's how it seems to Rhodes, particularly during the early days of the Arab Spring, when he can barely contain his excitement that this might be the change they can all believe in. He is unceasingly conscious of the importance of his work, and the potentially fateful consequences of a misstep. 'For me, this was a time when every moment had the electric charge

of history [...] Every statement we made, every meeting I
was in, every decision Obama had to make, felt like the most
important thing I'd ever been a part of – and I wanted us to do
something, to shape events instead of observing them.'

He wants to make a difference, but at the same time he
is terrified of getting it wrong. Rhodes can't stop worrying
about jumping the gun, fearful of putting words in the president's mouth that he can't take back. He remains traumatised
by an experience early in Obama's first presidential campaign,
when a remark he'd drafted for the inexperienced candidate
about being ready to go after bin Laden in Pakistan was condemned by the Pakistani leadership. The campaign's panicky
communications chief emailed Rhodes afterwards to tell him
that this was their worst mistake yet. 'I thought I'd tanked
the campaign,' Rhodes recalls of that miserable moment. 'A
knot formed in the pit of my stomach and tingled out into my
arms, a sense of stress that stayed with me for the next decade.'
Given that going after bin Laden in Pakistan would ultimately
help define Obama's time in office, there were plenty worse
mistakes he could have made than this one. But Rhodes should
also have known that almost nothing a would-be president says
about foreign policy has the power to do him terminal damage
anyway, because it doesn't matter enough. Only one truly
fateful thing was said during the 2008 campaign, and it came
from the lips of Obama's Republican opponent. After Lehman
Brothers went under in September, just seven weeks before
election day, 'John McCain uttered one of those phrases from
which presidential candidates never recover: "The fundamentals of the economy," he said, "are strong."' Rhodes was never
near enough to the things that really concerned the voters to
do Obama much harm, or much good, there.

What he did get to experience close up was Obama's
incredible pulling power internationally. To travel the globe
with the American president – and not just any president,
but *this* one – was to get access to some of the most famous

people in the world, who nevertheless continued to regard Obama with a kind of awe. Even as his popularity waned back home, Obama remained the biggest draw on the world stage. Stars were starstruck by him, and some of the fairy dust inevitably got sprinkled on whoever was standing nearby. Only on very rare occasions did someone manage to break the spell. In early 2011 Rhodes gets an invitation with the rest of Team Obama to a state banquet at Buckingham Palace. He rents a white-tie tuxedo – 'You guys clean up pretty well,' the impeccably turned-out Obama tells his normally scruffy speechwriters – and goes to see the British aristocracy put on a show. 'The women wore diamond tiaras; some of the men, military uniforms. One of these ladies, after telling me about her various hobbies, looked at me quizzically – "You do know who I am, don't you?" she said. *Of course*, I assured her […] I didn't have the slightest idea.' Then the real centre of attention arrives:

> Obama stood next to the queen, a stoic yet kindly-looking woman adorned in jewels. Standing there, you got the sense of the impermanence of your own importance – this woman had met everyone there was to know over the last fifty years […] When the dinner was over, we were moved to another room, where they served after-dinner drinks. I found myself in a conversation with David Cameron about the HBO show *Entourage*, which we both apparently enjoyed – in a room full of royals, the prime minister is oddly diminished, just another staffer.

'The Impermanence of Importance' is one of the brute facts of democratic life. The only people who rise above it are also the people who rise above politics.

||||
||||

In calling his book *The World As It Is*, Rhodes is referring to the ongoing contest between Obama's realism and his own hopes that the president would deliver lasting change. The tension between what is and what ought to be forms the essence of most political coming-of-age memoirs and this one is no different from other classics of the genre, such as *The Education of Henry Adams* (1918): the dilemmas it describes could come from any time in the history of modern politics, not just our own. But there is another reference point for the title, which exclusively concerns what is happening now. We are witnessing the increasingly fraught contest between the world as it is – the world of facts – and the world as it is described by people with little or no regard for the facts. Obama and Rhodes may sometimes have found themselves on different sides of the struggle between what is and what ought to be, but they were always on the same side of the struggle between the world as it is and the world as *they* say it is. Both men were victims of character assassinations by their opponents, who showed increasing disregard for anything that might be called common ground. During Obama's presidency the world as it is started to disappear, buried beneath the accusations and counter-accusations of those who said it was another way entirely, simply because they could.

This story is best told backwards, because it is a tale that culminates in the election of Trump. If that represented the ultimate catastrophe for Team Obama – 'after all the *work* you guys did,' Rhodes's wife says to him the morning after Trump's victory – what precedes it has to be sifted for clues that it might be coming. They are easy to miss, and Obama's people missed plenty of them at the time. Sometimes this was down to political incompetence, but there was also some arrogance. In April 2016 Obama travelled to London on a hastily arranged trip to help Cameron fight off the threat of defeat in the Brexit referendum. Obama is greeted by an op-ed from Boris Johnson in the *Telegraph* attacking him for removing a bust of Churchill from the Oval Office. 'Some said,' Johnson wrote, 'that it was a symbol of the part-Kenyan president's ancestral dislike of the British Empire.'

'Really?' Obama said. 'The black guy doesn't like the British?' We were standing in the US ambassador's house in London, a stately mansion with a lawn so big, with grass so carefully cut, that it resembled a football field without lines.

'They're more subtle back home,' I said.

'Not really,' he said. 'Boris is their Trump.'

Obama agreed to do what Cameron wanted, which was to explain that the Brexiteers' idea that they could easily negotiate a trade deal with the US was a fantasy. One of Cameron's people said: 'We'd be at the back of the queue.' Everyone laughed. 'It would be great,' Cameron said, 'if you could make that point publicly.' Obama did as he was asked. He also turned his fire on Johnson. 'As the first African-American president, it might be appropriate to have a bust of Dr Martin Luther King in my office to remind me of all the hard work of a lot of people who would somehow allow me to have the privilege of holding this office.'

Afterwards, Rhodes goes out to dinner with Cameron's team 'to celebrate a visit that had accomplished everything they had asked'. Nevertheless, the Americans are warned by the Brits that Brexit might still come to pass, if the voters decide they don't want to play it safe. Oh well, thinks Rhodes, Obama did what he could – he played the game, he delivered his bit, *he teed it up*. Except he didn't: he messed it up. Obama's visit was a drag on the Remain campaign, hampered by the obvious contrivance of his message. (By saying 'back of the queue' rather than 'back of the line' he made it clear he had been fed the quote by Cameron's people.) Campaigners for Vote Leave will still tell you that Obama's intervention was one of their best moments, because he was so tone-deaf to the dynamics of the referendum. He didn't notice how little most people cared about what he had to say; what bothered them was his presumption in coming all this way to say it. In some ways, there was a double complacency at work. Rhodes warns his British hosts in turn not to underestimate the threat posed by Trump. 'When I watch [Trump's] rallies,' he tells Cameron's people over dinner that night in their comfortable London restaurant, 'I think how potent his message would be from a more skilled politician.' The implication is that this form of politics might have its day one day, but not while the most skilful politician of all was still at the top of his game. How little they all knew.

Before Brexit, it was another B-word that signalled the dangers to come: Benghazi. After Chris Stevens, the US ambassador, was killed there in 2012 during an attack on the American compound, Hillary Clinton, as secretary of state, bore the brunt of Republican fury for what they saw as a cover-up of the truth. It became a matter of faith for many Republicans that the Obama administration had somehow been complicit in the attack, as revealed by their apparent refusal to condemn it as an act of terrorism. Rhodes, who was Obama's chief spokesman on the politics of the region, had met with Stevens shortly before his death to discuss how the US could help rebuild Libya's higher education system (it's hard to think of anything that would be more of a red rag to the bull of the alt-right than that idea). He soon got caught up in the madness that followed. It became the story that no one knew how to kill. '"Benghazi" was an accusation that seemed to mean everything and nothing at the same time, shifting from one conspiracy theory to the next.' Its ubiquity made Rhodes increasingly paranoid. 'Benghazi followed me around like an unseen shadow. When I met strangers, I wondered if they went home to Google me, only to find a litany of conspiracy theories.' It wasn't just people on the fringes who became obsessed with the issue. Even Mitt Romney, Obama's opponent in the 2012 presidential election, and in many ways a world-as-it-is Republican, couldn't resist the siren call of Benghazi.

It led to a moment that crystallised the way the political argument was changing. In 2012 Obama had struggled badly in his first presidential debate with Romney, coming across as world-weary and unengaged. Romney had been the more authoritative. For the second debate Obama's preparation was much more thorough, including on the matter of Benghazi. Fox News had run a relentless campaign claiming that Obama had refused to use the word 'terrorism' in his early responses to the attack. In fact, what Obama had said in the Rose Garden of the White House on the day after Stevens died was that it had been 'an act of terror'. His advisers, including Rhodes and chief speechwriter Jon Favreau, drummed into him that he must repeat this precise form of words, rather than getting sucked into calling it terrorism. They were laying a trap for Romney. In the debate Romney heard Obama claim that he had called Benghazi an 'act of terror'.

> Romney looked surprised, even shocked, at his good fortune. 'You said in the Rose Garden the day after the attack, it was an act of terror? It was not a spontaneous demonstration, is that what you are saying?'
>
> Obama was now the one who looked pleased. 'Please proceed, Governor,' Obama said.
>
> 'I want to make sure we get that for the record,' Romney said, 'because it took the president 14 days before he called the attack in Benghazi an act of terror.'
>
> 'Get the transcript,' Obama said.
>
> 'What an idiot,' Favreau said [of Romney], as we watched this unfold on a television backstage.

The debate moderator checks the transcript and confirms Obama is right. Romney can't believe it. Even though it is a decisive victory for his candidate, Rhodes still feels a chill. 'Romney

– an intelligent man – really did seem to believe something that wasn't true. You could almost see how his debate prep had gone, a group of aides who'd been feeding on a steady diet of Fox News […] I assumed they were just cynical; what if they actually believed this stuff?' With hindsight, the line that really stands out in that debate is 'Get the transcript.' That is so 2012. Who would think that the transcript would make any difference today?

|||||

But Rhodes's fears about what might be looming don't date back just to the 2012 election. They start in 2008. The politician who really scared him, and showed him what might be coming down the track, was Sarah Palin. When McCain chose her as his running mate, most Democrats treated it as an act of desperation – a Hail Mary pass, to use the sporting metaphor many favoured at the time. Rhodes is nowhere near so sanguine. Like McCain, he could immediately see that Palin's speech at the Republican convention was one of the best of the campaign. It electrified her audience, notwithstanding its lack of substance, and it fuelled their shared sense of grievance at Obama's rise. Even though Palin subsequently fell apart, Rhodes is still spooked by what he heard back then. In trying to describe his early misgivings, his normally assured prose style deserts him. 'As much as she became a punchline,' he writes, 'Palin's ascendance broke a seal on a Pandora's box: the innuendo and conspiracy theories that existed in forwarded emails and fringe right-wing websites now had a mainstream voice.' It's an ugly sentence, but its meaning is clear. When Trump wins the keys to the White House eight years later, the phrase that Rhodes uses to characterise the voters who put him there is telling. He calls them 'Palin's people'.

Was Obama sufficiently spooked? As the person at the eye of the storm, he does his level best not to let it get to him. From the outset he remained determined not to get dragged down by the craziness that surrounds his every move. This attitude plays to his strengths: his sangfroid is formidable, and his refusal to be baited is admirable. But it is also frustrating. It comes too close to that side of Obama's personality that ends up with him shrugging his shoulders and walking away. After Trump's victory, the Obama team convened a series of meetings to try to work out whether Russian interference in the election might have made the difference. Rhodes is tasked with bringing the president up to speed:

> I went to see Obama and told him that I thought we had a problem with Russia.
>
> 'You think?' he said sarcastically.
>
> 'I mean us. *We* have a problem. There's going to be a narrative,' I said, choosing my words carefully, 'that we didn't do enough. It's already building.'
>
> 'What were we supposed to do?' he asked. 'We warned people.'
>
> 'But people will say, why didn't we do more, why didn't you speak about it more?'
>
> 'When?' he asked. 'In the fall? Trump was already saying that the election was rigged.'
>
> I told him that I worried about the scale of the fake news effort, the disinformation that went beyond hacking. 'And do you think,' he asked me, 'that the type of people reading that stuff were going to listen to *me*?'

Of course, they weren't. But sometimes that's not the point. The point is you have to lay down a marker, so your own people know that you care.

Could things have been different? Rhodes doesn't have much time for what-ifs. Because his book is fixated on his relationship with the president, few other Democratic politicians get much of a look-in. Hillary appears in various walk-on parts, but Rhodes is so muted in how he talks about her it is hard to avoid the impression that he is trying not to talk about her at all.

An occasional but more vivid presence is Obama's vice-president, Joe Biden, who provides a glimpse of a different kind of politics. 'At 66, he was two decades older than Obama, and also embraced a more old-fashioned brand of politics – he'd walk through the hallways of the West Wing, stopping to talk to people, gripping your forearm and holding onto it as he spoke.' Here, again, is the ghost of LBJ. Though, as Biden has discovered, being a 'handsy' politician is not the free pass it once was.

Whereas Hillary offers advice that often seems technically correct but is painfully convoluted – of the Afghan war, she tells the president that 'putting in troops wouldn't work but still you need to put in troops' – Biden is much more direct, even if he is sometimes wrong. On Libya, he was probably right: when the White House was reviewing its options, Biden declared that to his mind 'intervention was, essentially, madness – why should we get involved in another war in a Muslim-majority country?' On the raid that resulted in the death of bin Laden, Biden was wrong: he warned Obama not to do it, because of the risk it would draw a military response from the Pakistanis. Hillary, by contrast, would only say that it was a 51:49 call. But even there, Biden comes out of the episode well. He tells Rhodes afterwards that he simply saw his job as making sure the president got enough robust advice that he had room to think for himself and wasn't captured by one side. After Obama had decided to go ahead, Biden was with him all the way. Once Biden was in, he was all in.

It is hard not to speculate about the what-ifs when reading about Biden. What if he had been the candidate in 2016? What if he had been the candidate in 2008, and Obama had been his running mate? What if Obama had tried occasionally to emulate Biden, rather than simply being grateful to have him around? When, two weeks before Trump's inauguration, James Comey and the other intelligence chiefs held a briefing for the outgoing administration on what they had learned about 'the relentless campaign waged by Putin on behalf of Trump', the

responses of the president and vice-president are a study in
their very different styles: 'Obama sat silent and stoic, occasionally asking questions for clarification. Biden was animated,
incapable of hiding his incredulity.' Sometimes, with Obama,
you feel a bit of incredulity might have done him some good.
But that wasn't his way.

One further calamity hangs over the story Rhodes has to
tell. It has nothing to do with Putin or Trump. Rhodes, who
often found he couldn't sleep ('the accumulated effect of
Benghazi stress and a hungry newborn'), binge-watches TV
through the night and becomes increasingly obsessed with his
favourite show, *Parts Unknown*, hosted by the chef Anthony
Bourdain. He sensed he had found another kindred spirit. 'I
felt a sense of recognition in this guy wandering around the
world, trying to find some temporary connection with other
human beings living within their own histories.' Rhodes makes
it one of his ambitions before leaving office to get Obama to
record an episode with Bourdain. Amazingly, he succeeds, and
on a trip to Vietnam in 2016 the two men are filmed sharing
a meal in a tiny restaurant, eating noodles while sitting on
plastic stools. Beforehand, Rhodes tries to explain to the president why he thinks he should do this. 'His philosophy isn't that
different from yours. If people would just sit down and eat
together, and understand something about each other, maybe
they could figure things out.' Obama recognises what Rhodes
is telling him. '"So we're doing this for you?" he laughed.'

In June 2018, just days after *The World As It Is* was published, Bourdain was found hanged in a hotel room in France,
having apparently killed himself in the middle of making an
episode of *Parts Unknown* in Strasbourg. It was a shocking,
inexplicable event. Obama immediately paid tribute, saying
that Bourdain's work had 'helped to make us a little less afraid
of the unknown'. Rhodes wrote: 'The curiosity, intelligence
and generosity of spirit in Anthony Bourdain's work got me
through some of the toughest times in the WH and opened

doors to new worlds.' These tributes were heartfelt, but they also felt inadequate, especially for Rhodes, given how much he had invested in what Bourdain had to offer. There was little consolation to be found here.

In the end, politics is not cooking. We have to do more than share a meal together. Nor is politics basketball. The team with the best player doesn't necessarily win. Politics isn't golf either. You can't just leave your opponents to play their game and hope you play yours better. What Rhodes and Obama had in common was that they were always looking for ways to make politics something other than it is: above all, to find some perspective on it with which they could feel more comfortable, or less than tormented. For Obama this was sometimes the grandest perspective of all. Late in his presidency he reads Yuval Harari's *Sapiens* and finds some consolation there, both in the idea that as a species what connects us are the stories we tell and also in the thought that none of us makes much difference overall: 'One thing he kept coming back to was the expanse of time, the fact that we were just "a blip" in human history.' Sometimes the comfort is to be found in the small world of family ties. On the flight back from one of his final overseas trips, he tells Rhodes: 'I am not certain of many things, but I am certain of one. On my deathbed, I won't be thinking about a bill I passed or an election I won or a speech I gave. I'll be thinking about my daughters and moments involving them.' I know it's true – at least, it is a truism – that no one passes their final moments wishing they had spent more time at the office. But still it is a little disappointing to have to hear it from the president of the United States, given what is at stake for all of us in the office he holds. Both Rhodes and Obama came into politics without deep party ties or a well-established political programme. Both were inexperienced. What they each had instead was enormous intelligence, along with a pronounced sense of right and a pronounced sense of self. It was too much, and it wasn't enough.

8

BLAIR REDUX

SINCE LEAVING OFFICE in 2007 Tony Blair has been busy hawking his wares around the world, from Nigeria to Kazakhstan. What has he been selling? Himself, of course, plus his reputation, and perhaps his party's too, somewhere down the river. But he's also been peddling an idea: deliverology. Here is the pitch, as described by Tom Bower. He reports Blair telling Paul Kagame, the Rwandan president, back in 2007: 'I learned by bitter experience during ten years as prime minister the problems of getting the government machine to deliver what I wanted. I created a Delivery Unit, and that was a great success. It transformed everything. I want to bring that success to Africa.' Or, as Blair put it to President Buhari of Nigeria at a meeting in 2015: 'I pioneered the skills to make government work effectively. The Delivery Unit is the leader's weapon to make his government effective across the civil service and country.' He offered to establish a delivery unit within Buhari's regime, staffed by experts from Blair's Africa Governance Initiative. At the same meeting, according to Bower, Blair asked the various aides present to leave the room so he could talk to the president alone. He told them he had a personal message to convey from David Cameron. In fact, he used the time to pursue some business on behalf of Tony Blair Associates, his commercial calling card. He wanted to sell the Nigerians

Israeli drones and other military equipment for use in their fight against Islamic rebels.

While he has been touting his achievements and his contacts overseas, Blair's popularity has cratered back at home. In a notably fractious age he has succeeded in uniting left and right of British politics against him. In mid-2018 his approval rating with the British public was at net minus 50 per cent, making him the least popular currently active political figure, on a par with Vladimir Putin and Donald Trump. Much of this animus is driven by continuing fury at his part in the Iraq War, along with distaste for the money Blair has made since leaving office (his net worth is estimated at £30–60 million). His repeated interventions on the issues of the day – telling the voters how misguided they are to have fallen for the idiocy of both Corbyn and Brexit – haven't helped. But all this irritation with post-prime minister Blair shouldn't distract from the problem with how ex-prime minister Blair now presents his time in office. Deliverology is itself a bogus prospectus. It relies on the assumption that Blair gradually mastered the skills needed to be an effective leader and that he was forced out just when he had got on top of the government machine. That's what he says in his memoirs, where he insists that he only worked out how to exercise power effectively towards the end of his time in office. Now he wants to help others start out with the wisdom he had to acquire through 'bitter experience'. But political leaders always say this: that governing starts to make sense when time is running out. That's one reason why it's so hard to persuade them to move on. In 2016 Obama told the podcaster Marc Maron that he was finally getting the hang of it seven and a bit years in, just when he had one foot out of the door. For democratic leaders this is the tragedy of power: they only learn how to do their jobs once the public is sick of the sight of them, or the constitution is telling them their time is up. But it's an illusion: it just seems easier because the end is in sight and they have stopped worrying about what might come next. Blair felt he was really getting things done at the point when his struggle with Gordon Brown was over. But it wasn't because he had worked out how to deal with an obstructive rival; it was because he had ultimately been defeated by him. He was liberated by having little left to lose. Delivery depends much more on context than it does on technique. In that respect, it's not a transferable skill.

When Blair says he can provide Kagame with a weapon to use across the civil service and the country, it doesn't mean what it would mean in a British context. Blair's domestic beef was with a civil service that he felt had become entrenched and hidebound, an obstacle in the way of reform. But what about countries where the civil service barely functions, where the rule of law is at best an aspiration and leaders deploy real weapons against their own people as well as metaphorical ones? The deliverologists would say it is even more important to have clear targets and a separate machinery for achieving them when the rest of the government is corrupt and inefficient. But establishing that sort of personal remit under the leader's authority isn't just a matter of efficiency; it is also a question of power. Bypassing the civil service does nothing to stop power being abused; if anything, the reverse is true. Kagame's regime has become notorious for its brutal suppression of opposition forces; murders and disappearance are routine. Kagame amended the constitution to allow him to run for another three terms in office, meaning he could potentially stay on until 2034. Blair says that he makes sure to raise what he calls 'the human rights stuff' whenever he is pushing his delivery agenda in parts of the world where democratic institutions are fragile. But he doesn't feel he can do more than that, given that target-setting is where he can make a real difference. That's the promise of deliverology: to carve out a space separate from the messy business of politics, where different rules apply. Carving out a separate space for government is attractive for political leaders of all stripes because it

frees them from the normal limitations of rule-governed politics. It is dangerous precisely because it is so unconstrained.
That's why the step from selling deliverology to selling arms is
a relatively short one.

In marshalling the case against Blair's globetrotting activities, Bower seems unsure what the central charge against his
subject is. Was the problem with Blair that he was a deliverologist who failed to deliver? Or is deliverology itself the problem,
a pseudo-philosophy of government that ends up being about
everything and nothing? This confusion permeates Bower's
account of the central failure of Blair's time in office: the Iraq
War. Here, though, the picture is further complicated by a third
possibility: was Blair just posing as a deliverologist when in
fact he was an ideologue all along? Bower marshals everything
that can be said against the Iraq catastrophe, from doctored
dossiers to cavalier disregard for the rule of international law.
He quotes General Mike Jackson, who toured Basra in May
2003 after the victory over Saddam. 'It is startlingly apparent,'
Jackson reported to London, 'that we are not delivering that
which was deemed to be promised and is expected.' Jackson
was encouraged to keep his concerns to himself, since this was
meant to be a good news story – Victory! – and nothing was
to be done to rock the boat. What are we meant to conclude
from this: that if the Blair government had been more focused
on delivering what was promised and less on managing the
headlines, the war could have been a success? Was it therefore a failure of planning? Or was it a far deeper moral failure,
because the British government could never have delivered on
its promises to the people of Iraq? And if so, was that because
Blair's inner circle was thinking only about news management,
or because news management was itself in the service of a
neoconservative agenda that was impervious to the evidence?
Bower mocks Blair for spending his time reading the Quran
instead of studying policy papers that might have given him a
better understanding of recent Middle Eastern history and the

Shia / Sunni conflicts that cut across it. This Blair is the opposite of a deliverologist: he is more like a mystic. Yet he is the same Blair whom Bower accuses of having no sense of purpose: a grinning fool he derides for prancing around his Downing Street flat in his yellow and green underpants.

||||
||||

The truth is that Blair was all these people and more: the mystic, the fool, the sofa politician, the neocon, the preacher on a tank and the deliverologist. The reason the last matters is that it allowed Blair to play all the other roles as well. Deliverology might be designed to pin the civil service down, but it frees the politician up. Targets sound constraining when they are in fact liberating, because they can be put in the service of an ideology or they can just as well stand in place of one. Deliverology allowed Blair to follow his whims, which took him all over the map. What it didn't do was force him to face up to his weaknesses as a politician. These included his lack of historical perspective and his craven inability to face down Gordon Brown. When Blair met a barrier in the way of something he wanted to do, he swerved, taking his targets with him. Bower quotes Robin Butler, Blair's first cabinet secretary, saying of his earliest official encounter with the newly elected prime minister: 'He's scared of me. He didn't even ask me how to make the government machine work.' In truth, Blair was scared of the hard work involved in getting the civil service on his side. He was always looking for short cuts. The result was an administration whose permanently aggrieved sense of having to operate in a hostile institutional environment became a self-fulfilling prophecy. The British civil service may have many failings, but if you want to deliver lasting change it is the only instrument that can do it for you. Blair treated the administrative machinery of the UK state as though he really were in Africa, with predictably counterproductive results. This was why he was so prone to call in the army, as during the fuel crisis of 2000 and the foot-and-mouth crisis of 2001. Once a mess of his own making had been solved by a flex of authoritarian muscle, Blair asked his advisers: 'Why can't all government be as successful as this?' If he needed to ask, he was never going to be satisfied with the answer.

The other recurring charge against Blair, both during his time in office and subsequently, is that he confused politics with celebrity. Or, to put in more bluntly, that he got drunk on wealth and fame. Bower's other biographical subjects have tended to be larger-than-life figures from the business, sports and showbiz worlds, for whom fame and money are more or less interchangeable: Robert Maxwell, Mohammed Al-Fayed, Conrad Black, Bernie Ecclestone, Simon Cowell. Blair is in a very different line of business, but it is striking how often his world overlaps with Bower's more usual hunting ground. My favourite moment comes at a dinner Blair hosted at Chequers in 2006:

> Big Ken Anderson [a Texan consultant hired in 2002 to sort out costs in the NHS] gave it to Blair straight: 'There's been a lot of pushback by the civil service,' he said. 'Ultimately, however you measure it, it's all been a failure.' Blair flashed with silent dismay. Hearing the truth was unpleasant. With Elton John, another guest, seated nearby, there was no opportunity for a proper discussion but Anderson's views on the NHS were no secret. Blair's reforms were grinding to a halt.

Indeed, it must be hard to have a serious policy discussion when Elton John will keep popping up at the wrong moment. Bower is good at capturing both the inadvertent humour and the inadvertent horror of the netherworld in which Blair came to move, an uneasy mixture of celebrity, charity and wonkery. Blair's post-2007 career has allowed him to indulge all his worst instincts in these directions, along with his burning desire to make a lot of money, which seems to have been there all along. However, he hasn't had it all his own way. Bower recounts what happened when Blair bumped up against another of his favourite subjects, the notorious do-gooder and skinflint Richard Branson. As a 'face for hire' providing consultancy advice for various 'green' ventures, Blair offered his services to Branson, who was dabbling in this area. 'Almost inevitably,' Bower writes, 'Blair accepted Branson's invitations to visit Necker, part of the British Virgin Islands, but eventually discovered that the tycoon refused to reimburse him for advice.' Maybe there is no such thing as a free holiday after all.

However, the truly scary parts of Bower's story don't really concern Blair at all, or his intimate circle, or even his ever growing property empire or his flirtations with the international arms trade. It comes when he strays into the orbit of the post-presidential Bill Clinton, who has long inhabited the same netherworld in which he now operates. Blair hooked up with Branson via Clinton, whose foundation has its finger in many of the same pies that Blair has been trying to access on the speechmaking/fundraising/deal-brokering circuit. More than once, as I read Bower on Blair the international deliverologist, I found myself wondering what a no-holds-barred exposé of the Clinton Foundation over the same period would look like. It was a chilling thought. As Hillary Clinton squared off against Trump for the presidency in 2016, those fears came to seem more and more pressing. Hillary Clinton should have been able to defeat Trump fairly easily, other things being equal. But other things were not equal. The way Tony Blair and Bill Clinton have conducted themselves since leaving office has long been a hostage to the fortunes not just of their personal reputations but also of the centrist political causes they continue to represent. It is sometimes said that Clinton and Blair should shoulder the blame for making politicians like Jeremy Corbyn and Bernie Sanders so appealing to their erstwhile supporters. But that's probably as it should be: political parties move on. The true scandal of deliverology would come if it helped to deliver the election of President Trump. And it did.

9

DAVID CAMERON

ARE YOU A TEAM PLAYER or are you a wanker? In a world that divides between the people who divide it in two and those who don't, David Cameron sits squarely in the former camp. During the summer of 2014 he was putting the finishing touches to a government reshuffle that would see him shunt his old friend Michael Gove from the Department of Education to a new role as chief whip. This was at best a sideways move for Gove, if not an outright demotion. Cameron was clearing the decks for the following year's election and he needed one of his most contentious and least popular ministers to be less visible. Still, he discussed it with Gove beforehand – selling it as an opportunity to put 'all that passion and antagonism' to better use – and he thought he had his friend's agreement. Then, out of the blue, 'Michael emailed to say he had changed his mind.' Cameron responded with raw fury. 'I smelt Dominic Cummings,' he says now, 'and totally flipped.' He called Gove to say that he refused to accept his email and was holding him to his previous agreement to take the job. He followed this up with a text. 'You must realise I divide the world into team players and wankers. You've always been a team player. Please don't become a wanker.' Cameron does not tell us how Gove responded, but he was in post as chief whip by the following day. However, Cameron was not enough of a team player himself to appreciate that along with a £36,000 pay cut Gove was also being asked to accept a change of status, since the chief whip only attends cabinet, rather than being a full member. Gove was deeply resentful. His wife, the *Daily Mail* journalist Sarah Vine, was absolutely livid. 'I had created a strong team,' Cameron writes, 'but tensions and unhappiness were on the rise and the long-term consequences would be very serious indeed.'

The bubbling resentments in Cameron's relationship with Gove, whom he liked and whose company he enjoyed but whom he never quite trusted, is a recurrent theme in Cameron's account of his time at the top. Gove, Cameron can't resist pointing out, was the only one of his close allies who strongly advised him against running for the Tory leadership in 2005. He also recounts a testy cabinet meeting at which Gove and William Hague clashed about the government's response to the Arab Spring – Gove wanting to take the side of freedom, Hague preferring caution. What struck Cameron wasn't the argument but the fact that it made its way into the next day's papers, 'something that often seemed to happen when Michael was involved.' Cameron complains repeatedly about Gove's tendency to go off-piste and off message, whether by sermonising in cabinet and or by writing tendentious newspaper articles that went well beyond his brief. He offended Cameron in March 2014 when in an interview with the *Financial Times* he called the number of Old Etonians at No. 10 'preposterous', following Jo Johnson's promotion to be head of the Policy Unit. Always in the background lurked Gove's friend and adviser Cummings, whom Cameron suspects of whispering poison into his master's ear. Things finally came to a head in 2016, when Gove went to see Cameron and George Osborne in Cameron's Downing Street flat and told them that he was considering siding with the Brexiteers in the forthcoming referendum. He had yet to finally make up his mind but as he explained: 'If I do decide to opt for Brexit, I'll make one speech. That will be it. I'll play no further part in the campaign.' Cameron was dumbfounded.

I found it hard to believe what was happening. Michael was a close confidant. Part of my inner team. Someone I often turned to for advice. Why hadn't he told me before that this might happen? Of course I understood his strong Euroscepticism, but if he was undecided – and it sounded like a 50–50 call for him – wouldn't his loyalty be the thing that brought him down on one side or the other? Not personal loyalty to me, but loyalty to the team, to the project, to the future of our party and our country. But if he was really going to do this, back Brexit, then I believed him – really believed him – when he said he'd take a back seat.

This, of course, is the ultimate betrayal. Gove did not take a back seat. He made many more than one speech. Where he led, Boris Johnson followed. The rest is history. So much for being part of the team.

||||
||||

Cameron experienced a similar sense of bemusement and betrayal in his dealings with another person who was instrumental in persuading the British electorate to vote for Brexit. Paul Dacre, editor of the *Daily Mail*, ran a ferociously pro-Leave campaign despite his newspaper's never previously having argued for quitting the EU. Cameron invited him to the Downing Street flat to explain himself. Dacre said that the *Mail* had always been a pretty Eurosceptic paper, to which Cameron responds that he had always been a pretty Eurosceptic prime minister – but that didn't mean he had to argue to leave. Anyway, Cameron wanted to know, if Dacre was such a devoted Brexiteer, why had he backed Ken Clarke to be leader of the Conservative Party? But Cameron knew that expecting consistency from the *Mail* is like expecting loyalty from Boris Johnson. So he turned his attentions to Dacre's boss, the

Mail's owner Lord Rothermere, who also got invited round for a drink. Could he not see that however frustrating it was to be in the EU, it would be worse to be out? Rothermere's response was that he thought things were far more serious than that. But instead of the expected diatribe against Brussels, he told Cameron: 'I think it will be a disaster if we leave. I may even have to relocate some of my businesses to be inside the EU.' With hindsight, Cameron has some regrets about what happened next.

> It has been reported that I went on to ask him to sack Paul Dacre. Frankly, I wish I had – and I wish it had happened. I suspect he does too: two years after the referendum he replaced Dacre with the pro-Remain Geordie Greig. The closest I got was saying: 'Well if that's your view, why on earth have you got someone editing the *Daily Mail* who is determined to drive us out of the EU?' There was a lot of harrumphing about not instructing editors, and we left it at that. The *Mail* had made its choice.

Wankers.

It's probably true that Cameron had little leverage left over tabloid editors and their proprietors, especially in the aftermath of the Leveson inquiry, which had poisoned relations between the press and politicians. But Gove is another story. Someone close to that 2016 meeting between Gove, Cameron and Osborne once told me that it was the moment when the Remain campaign was lost – or at least when the chance of an easy victory was squandered. On this account, Gove had gone along in the clear expectation that Cameron would strike a hard deal – that if Gove was insistent on campaigning for Brexit, his boss would insist in return that he resign from the government. The price of being allowed to remain in his job would be to make one speech and leave it at that. He could vote for Brexit if he wanted but he couldn't lead the charge for it. If he broke those rules, he would be fired. In other words, Gove was expecting Cameron to be the one who made him take a back seat. Moreover, he was apparently prepared to accept the deal – he would agree to keep quiet if the price of speaking out was to be kicked out of Cameron's team. Gove also knew that if he didn't take the lead then Johnson would be reluctant to put his own head above the parapet. So leadership of the Brexit campaign would fall by default to Farage, who had no such scruples, and almost no chance of winning it on his own. All of this is what Gove expected to happen and it is what he had reconciled himself to. But Cameron never made the ask. Instead, once he discovered that Gove was thinking of abandoning him, he simply showed his disdain. In the version I was given, Cameron was portrayed as just too posh to sully himself with threats and blandishments towards a man he considered his social inferior. This is surely a caricature. But another way to put it is that he was trapped by his binary view of political character. Once Gove stopped being a team player, he revealed himself as a wanker. Cameron seemingly had no room for people who might be neither. Or who, perhaps, might find a way to be both.

Cameron could argue – though he doesn't in his memoir – that by letting members of his cabinet campaign against the government's position while keeping their jobs he was following the precedent set by Harold Wilson in the 1975 referendum, when the same thing happened. But precedent doesn't count for much with referendums, since there are very few fixed requirements. Each one is its own distinctive struggle and the rules often get made up as you go along. The other side – including Cummings, chief strategist of the Vote Leave campaign – understood this. Part of Cameron's problem is that he was excessively influenced by his experience of the 2014 Scottish independence referendum, when he put his premiership on the line for another knife-edge, in/out, winner-take-all vote, and won. But the Brexit referendum was different and in refusing to acknowledge the differences Cameron ended up losing everything. As far as I can see, two things went wrong. In one crucial respect, Cameron failed to follow the winning formula that served him so well in Scotland. Separately, and more significantly, he failed to appreciate that an in/out vote, which suited his purposes in Scotland, was a big mistake for the question of EU membership. This mistake didn't just cost Cameron his political career. It cost the country its political sanity in the years that followed.

||||
||||

His sin of omission was his refusal to do with Brexit what he did in the final week of the Scottish referendum, when the real fear he might lose persuaded him to make concessions to the arguments of the other side. Cameron has confessed that in his alarm in the days before the Scottish vote, he asked the Queen to 'raise an eyebrow' to indicate her displeasure at the thought that the Union might dissolve. This plea came immediately after the appearance of the first poll to have the Independence campaign in the lead, which Cameron says 'hit him like a blow to the solar plexus'. If nothing else, getting the monarch involved shows that Cameron was perfectly prepared to make up his own rules when it suited him. We have no way of knowing if the Queen's intervention – gently asking people, on her way to church, to 'think very carefully about the future' – made any difference. What does seem to have really helped was the pledge delivered by the three main Westminster party leaders – Cameron, Miliband and Clegg – to devolve more powers to Holyrood in the event of a 'No' vote and to wrap this up in a generous offer of future funding.

Until that point, the focus of the 'No' campaign had been on the risks of independence. The message was: don't chance it! But in the last week of the campaign the emphasis shifted to what might be motivating people's desire to leave and finding ways to address it. Project Fear became Project We Hear You. That never happened with Brexit. It was discussed. The problem was that it would mean making a last-ditch pledge on immigration and Cameron didn't want to go down that road. Nor did his chief campaign strategist Lynton Crosby, who kept coming back to the importance of message discipline on the economy. 'All Leave has is immigration,' Crosby told Cameron. 'We shouldn't concede that it is the only battle to be fought.' Crosby wasn't involved in the Scottish referendum. If he had been, he might have accepted that when the other side are winning with what they have, making concessions to their arguments may be the only thing you have left.

There was no single shock poll before Brexit that panicked the main party leaders into action. Instead, the late blow to the solar plexus came in the form of an unprecedented act of political violence: the assassination of the Labour MP Jo Cox, killed a week before polling day by a man who shouted 'Britain first' as he carried out the attack. The effect of this terrible event was the opposite of galvanising. It froze the campaign in place, with politicians unable or unwilling to change tack in its aftermath. Those on the Remain side appeared to conclude there was nothing to be gained by pandering to the views of their opponents. Better just to keep insisting they knew better. When the campaign resumed, Cameron writes:

> We were still waking up each morning to the views of the latest expert or industry on the merits of Remain. I thought it was one of our great advantages that nearly every voice that mattered backed our case. The voice of major industries: cars, planes, trains, food, pharmaceuticals, farming, fashion, film. The voice of business: the CBI. The voice of many workers: the TUC. Our allies around the world: America, India, Japan, Australia, Canada. The multilateral bodies of the world: the IMF, the WTO, the OECD. Thirteen Nobel Prize winners.

The head of the NHS. The formers heads of MI5 and
MI6. Nine out of ten economists. Stephen Hawking, Tim
Berners-Lee and Richard Branson – truly great Britons
who so many people admire and respect. 'Maybe it's
a conspiracy,' I would say. 'Or maybe these people are
right.'

This is disingenuous. First, the case being made was rarely
about the merits of Remain; it was more often about the folly
of Leave. Second, if one Nobel Prize winner isn't enough, then
twelve more won't make much difference: either people are
listening or they are not. Finally, calling this the list of 'nearly
every voice that mattered' shows what's wrong with it. It does
not read like a litany of diverse perspectives. Rather it's a set of
people united by their sense of what they have to lose. These
voices, even if they come from across the world, still share a
worldview, underpinned by higher education, metropolitan
values and overlapping connections. (The exception is the
TUC, but the union movement was more divided on Brexit
than Cameron allows here.) Maybe it's not a conspiracy. But it
still looks like a cosy club; or perhaps, as Cameron would say,
a team.

||||

Critics have pointed out that Cameron himself has barely a
good word to say for the EU throughout his account of his
time in office, yet at the end he expects people to vote to stay
in it. In his own mind, as he explained to Dacre, these positions are compatible: deep Euroscepticism was consistent
with acknowledging that life would be worse on the outside.
Yet this gets to the heart of what was wrong with Cameron's
approach. He was in the business of trying to get a different
deal for Britain in Europe: to stay in, yes, but also to become
more detached, with increasing opt-outs and vetoes as part of

a looser, less federalist, more multi-track organisation. He still insists that he was serious about renegotiating a new arrangement before putting the question of continued membership to the people in a referendum. He regrets he didn't get a better deal in his battles with Merkel and Juncker but argues it was not for want of trying. But the sequencing here is back to front. Renegotiation then referendum was Cameron's mantra. That was never going to work. The referendum had to come before the renegotiation if he was going to have a stick to beat the Europeans with. That meant the referendum couldn't be an in/out one. It had to be on something the EU was demanding of Britain: a new treaty, perhaps, or some wider vision of the future relationship. Then, if the British people said no to what was on offer – which they likely would – Cameron would have been in a position to strike a really hard bargain. In this respect, a vote on the UK's membership of the EU was nothing like the case of Scottish independence. There, Cameron was all for the status quo. He took a gamble that he could defend the status quo in a straight shoot-out with the radical alternative. It also meant he was willing to concede bits of the status quo in a last-ditch effort to save it. With the EU, Cameron hated the status quo. He wanted to change it. In those circumstances, an in/out referendum was the last thing he should have risked.

This becomes clear when Cameron describes the long history of other people's demands for a referendum on Europe, well before he finally granted one. He is rightly resentful of the idea that he called the Brexit vote simply to resolve an internal Tory Party dispute. As he says, if that were true, then why had all the main political parties – including Labour and the Liberal Democrats – gone into general elections over the previous decade promising an EU referendum? Plus, he adds, if he were simply pandering to Eurosceptic opinion in his own party, he had no need to call an in/out vote. 'If it was only about managing the party, I could have come up with a formulation for a different sort of referendum, rather than a full in/out version. A nationwide plebiscite asking for a fundamental change in Britain's relationship with Europe – a so-called "mandate referendum" – was popular at the time with some of the party's leading Eurosceptics.' But that line of defence begs the obvious question: why then did he plump for the straight in/out choice? Just because he'd rejected devo max in the Scottish case was not a reason to reject it here. After all, in this case it was precisely what he wanted: maximum devolved power from Europe.

Even Bill Cash, the most die-hard Eurosceptic of them all, had in 2011 advocated a three-way choice in any referendum: between stay, leave and 'renegotiate'. Cameron says of his thinking in 2012, when he first started seriously to contemplate the need to hold an EU referendum, that 'when the inevitable new treaty came [it] meant we'd have to hold a referendum – and the pressure for an in/out one would be huge.' But would it? The three main parties had all gone into the 2005 general election promising not an in/out vote but a referendum on the Constitutional Treaty. The fact that Blair and then Brown never delivered on this promise as the Constitutional Treaty turned into the Lisbon Treaty did not invalidate it. Yes, there was mounting pressure to hold a referendum and yes, previous pledges to hold one had not been honoured. But none of that made it necessary for Cameron go the whole hog with in/out. Clear-sighted Tory Eurosceptics understood this. One said as much in a *Daily Telegraph* article back in June 2012. 'The fact is that the British people are not happy with what they have, and neither am I. That's why … the problem with an in/out referendum is that it offers a single choice, whereas what I want – and what I believe the vast majority of the British people want – is to make changes to our relationship.' The author? David Cameron.

Of course, some people have always vociferously advocated a straight choice between stay or leave. These include Nigel Farage and UKIP, but they also included the Lib Dems.

Among the many puzzling features of recent politics is that Jo Swinson, the Lib Dem leader in the 2019 general election, was a ferocious critic of Cameron's decision to call the referendum, even though she, like Nick Clegg and the rest of her party, had been arguing for an in/out vote on Europe back in 2009. How to explain it? Well, what's the one thing Ukippers and Lib Dems have in common? Neither of them is in the business of renegotiating Britain's relationship with the EU. In the one case that's because they don't want a relationship. In the other it's because they are happy with the relationship we have and want to recommit to it. In/out is the preferred option of the non-negotiators. Moreover, they are right to prefer it, since it represents a terrible basis for any negotiation. If we choose to stay we have nothing to negotiate with. And if we choose to leave we have nothing to negotiate with. Cameron's initial miscalculation was to assume, as he did back in 2012, that another new treaty was inevitable and that he could have his referendum on that. But when no new treaty was forthcoming, he compounded his error by insisting on a referendum anyway, though there was nothing left but membership or non-membership to vote on. As a result, he got himself in entirely the wrong camp for his purposes. He ended up siding with the position of the Europhobes in UKIP and the most Europhile of Lib Dems, instead of with the pragmatists, one of whom he had once been.

One of the few people who tried to warn Cameron off the referendum was his most trusted ally, George Osborne. It is one of the ironies of this story that Cameron ended up doing something that Clegg, whom he had no reason to follow, had once wanted, while ignoring the advice of his closest confidant Osborne, someone Cameron describes as 'more politically astute that anyone I have ever met'. Osborne told Cameron that the problem with the referendum – or 'your fucking referendum,' as he was later to call it – was that the government had no basis to secure the necessary concessions from Brussels beforehand, with the result that the timing was all wrong. Osborne was right about that. He was right about other things too, often enough to bear out something of Cameron's description of him. Osborne helped save Cameron's skin in 2007, when Gordon Brown had just become PM and was contemplating a snap general election that might have ended Cameron's career. The shadow chancellor came to the rescue by devising a series of counter-measures that stopped Brown in his tracks, including an announcement on raising the inheritance tax threshold that brought the aged delegates at the Tory Party conference to their feet. This had the double advantage of spooking Brown while providing Cameron with a commitment to which he need not feel fully committed and could readily bargain away in his negotiations with the Lib Dems during the formation of the coalition, which is what he did. Likewise, it was Osborne who calculated that making the Conservatives the party of austerity going into the 2010 election would blunt Brown's usual line of attack that the Tories had a secret agenda of welfare cuts. If it wasn't a secret, what was there to attack?

Osborne held his nerve in 2012, when the government's economic program looked to be seriously off track and his own political reputation was at a low ebb following the 'Omnishambles' budget that spring. He gambled that by 2015 job creation and an uptick in economic growth would override memories of the government's incompetence and compensate for the effects of austerity among those parts of the electorate the Conservatives needed to reach. As a governing strategy it was socially divisive and politically risky; it was also highly effective. Osborne's strategic nous stands in stark contrast to the almost comical ineptitude shown by Clegg, Cameron's deputy PM, who emerges from Cameron's account as one of the least politically astute people you will ever meet. Osborne frequently ran rings round him. Worse, he occasionally tried to save him from himself, though Clegg was either too puffed up or too pre-occupied to take the advice he was given. Osborne knew full well that junior partners in governing coalitions can face electoral ruin unless they tread very carefully. He thought Clegg should know it too, but Clegg seemed to prefer wishful thinking. The perfect vignette of this comes on the day when Clegg tells Cameron and Osborne, to their considerable astonishment, that he is going to support the government on tuition fees, despite having made a personal and manifesto commitment to do no such thing.

> George did something surprising. 'Don't do it,' he told Nick. 'It would be a huge political mistake for you.'
>
> George's concern for Nick was genuine. And he worried about the health of the coalition if one partner damaged itself like this.
>
> I saw it differently. 'George makes a good point, but I want us to do things together,' I said. 'And this is the right thing to do.'
>
> Nick was adamant: 'Our old policy was wrong; this is a good policy.'
>
> It was one of the bravest steps I have ever seen a politician take.

There you have it: Nick was brave but wrong; George was calculating but correct; Dave could see that George was probably right; but more important for Dave, Nick was being a good team player; even if that meant he was destroying himself and ultimately the team.

||||
||||

Once it became clear in the run-up to the 2015 election that the Lib Dems were in deep trouble, Cameron was as content as Osborne to try to put them out of business. He could comfort himself with the thought that it was Clegg's wider miscalculations that had left him staring at the abyss. It started with the referendum on the Alternative Vote, which Clegg had negotiated as a halfway-house option during the formation of the coalition government. His first mistake was to have fatally misjudged the extent of cross-party support for the change. Clegg thought something short of full-blown PR would be easier for the others to get behind. It turned out simply to be easier for them to neglect. When the vote came in 2011 cross-party support was non-existent – the Tories didn't want it, and were willing to use Clegg's agonies over tuition fees to discredit it, and Labour saw no reason to help. Clegg's halfway house proved to be his ruin. Then, increasingly frustrated with the lack of progress on constitutional reform, he decided to block the Tory plan to redraw constituency boundaries, which had been intended to correct what was seen as an anti-Tory bias. This act of sabotage should have made it more difficult for the Tories to win a majority at the next election. But instead it persuaded the Tories that they had nothing to lose by targeting every Lib Dem seat they could. Finally, with his options running out, Clegg chose to pin his hopes on helping his MPs defend their seats using the advantage of incumbency. He believed that even if his party's national vote share fell dramatically, he could hold on to enough locally popular sitting MPs to form another coalition. He went into the 2015 election with 57 MPs. He came out with eight. To general astonishment – perhaps even including Osborne's – the Tories had their overall majority, thanks to the efforts of their hapless coalition partners.

Even if much of this was ultimately Osborne's strategy, it needed Cameron to sell it. Both men understood he was by far the better frontman. He seems genuinely to have believed in the coalition for as long as it lasted: he liked the idea of holding together a disparate team. It is telling that he begins his memoir with the story of how the coalition was formed over five days in May 2010 and still takes pride in it as his greatest achievement. He was also better than Osborne would have been at concealing the political calculation that ultimately lead to its demise. Cameron was able both to cherish and to put the boot into the coalition at the same time. He was a many-faced politician, leading a many-faced party at the head of a many-faced government, which meant he was particularly well-suited to keeping the show on the road. He knows this about himself. He says he was never the stand-out among his Conservative contemporaries at any particular aspect of the political arts: not as astute as Osborne; not as far-sighted about the need for change as Michael Portillo; not as oratorically gifted as Hague. But he was enough of all these things to be the one true leader among them. It is also striking that for someone who is so keen to divide the world up in two, he recognised that his style of political leadership was anything but binary. He calls himself, with only a hint of vanity, a 'political decathlete, switching from one discipline to the next and trying to give every single one of them [my] best.'

Much of what he relished about being prime minister – and he clearly did relish it – was the range of tasks it demanded of him, from mundane party management to high political gossip, from the grandest foreign trips to the most routine constituency visits, from interpreting economic forecasts to summarising legal briefs, from dealing with terrorists to dealing with his colleagues. He is determined to recount it all and to remind us of everything that went to make up his premiership: the Leveson inquiry, the Saville inquiry, Syria, Libya, riots, 'plebgate', the Olympics, China, Russia, Afghanistan (on which, he somewhat surprisingly says, 'I spent more time – visiting, reading, discussing, deliberating, and yes worrying – than on any other issue'), aircraft carriers, university funding, 'free' schools, corporation tax, the 'bedroom' tax, the Bank of England, the 'special relationship', Stormont, Holyrood, Balmoral, and on, and on. We get it: it wasn't all Brexit. The political decathlete wants us to know it's not just about what happens in the last race.

He had other strengths too. He seems to have been good at taking criticism, especially from his wife Samantha, who emerges as the unsung hero of his tale. It was she who told him he was 'hopeless' following the first prime ministerial debate in 2010 and made him watch the whole thing again so he could improve next time – both of which he did. He didn't always listen to her: in 2003 she told him that he was absolutely wrong to back the Iraq war and that he would regret not sticking to his initial scepticism. She didn't enjoy her husband being PM nearly as much as he did. He describes a trip to Washington DC for an official visit with the Obamas: Cameron's 'idea of heaven' was her 'version of hell'. The only way she could get through it was with the help of vodka and painkillers. But she shared in the pleasure of his victories and felt fully the misery of his defeats. There are two photos, one taken of the pair of them watching the results as they come in on the night of his greatest triumph, the 2015 election, the other doing the same on the night of his greatest disaster, the Brexit referendum. In the first she looks the more elated; in the second, the more despondent. Still, as Cameron says of their relationship, especially when he movingly describes the short life of their son Ivan, politics was not the main thing anyway.

Cameron also has plenty of blind spots. He prides himself on his far greater openness to appointing women to important positions than any of his predecessors, including his ultimate hero, Margaret Thatcher. He boasts that by the time he left office nearly half of all his special advisors were female. He deeply resents the idea that he was running a 'chumocracy', which is one reason why Gove's jibe about the Old Etonian coterie at No. 10 really hit home. Yet it is noticeable that, with the exception of his wife and Angela Merkel, almost all the important conversations he recounts are with men. Women are often present, but usually in the background, and sometimes they are not there at all. When he first assembles his core team of parliamentary supporters for his 2005 bid to become Conservative leader, he is delighted by the fact that 'they were just the sort of people I wanted: bright, sane, forward-looking ...' He proudly lists all fourteen of them; they are all men.

But the person who is really missing from Cameron's version of his life in politics is his successor. He barely mentions her, even after he appointed her as his home secretary in 2010. He does spend quite a lot of time describing the changes he decided were needed to make the Tories electable again, once he had arrived in Parliament back in 2001 and discovered the unreconstructed state they were in. He concluded that the party needed to soften its image, to have more women MPs, and to be more open to innovation in state education. Theresa May thought the same, and acted on these thoughts well before Cameron did. But from this book you wouldn't know she was there at all. No wonder she ended up despising Cameron and what he stood for.

In many ways the oddity is that Cameron managed to retain his non-binary view of politics when he had such a binary view of other people. And it's not just his fellow politicians that he sorts into team players and the rest – it's also society as a whole. He talks repeatedly about British society being broken and of the need he felt to fix it. When riots broke out across England in the summer of 2011 he says it confirmed him in his view that this is a 'broken society,' something he claims his Lib Dem partners in coalition were too 'squeamish' to admit. This is absurd: if politics can be multi-faceted then so too can everything else. Society does not have to be either broken or fixed: it can be both and it can be neither. In the end, Cameron says of his time in government:

> We proved in an increasingly polarised age that politics wasn't either/or – you could be pro-defence and pro-aid; pro-family and pro-equality; pro-public services and pro-fiscal prudence too. We demonstrated that you could

take the difficult decisions *and* win elections – and that a government could achieve a lot in just six years.

Well, it's not just politics that doesn't have to be either/or. But that's not the point. Given what he says here, why on earth did he turn British politics into just another either/or question? It was a crazy thing to do. Given all these other things he says he achieved, it is understandable that he does not want Brexit to be his legacy. But thanks to the choice he made, it is.

10

THERESA MAY

THERESA MAY GREW UP in a Cotswold village called Church Enstone, where her father was vicar for much of the 1960s. The vicarage is within five miles of what became David Cameron's constituency home when he was MP for Witney. It is roughly the same distance from what is now Soho Farmhouse, a private club that serves as a little piece of the metropolis for the Chipping Norton set. Cameron is a member there too. It is unlikely May has ever been inside. May's maternal and paternal grandmothers were both in service, and one of her great-grandfathers was a butler. As Rosa Prince writes in her 2017 pop-up biography of May, Cameron's ancestors 'were more likely to employ maids than to work as servants'. Prince doesn't need to spell the moral out: once upon a time, not so very long ago, May might have been Cameron's maidservant. Two stories, two different worlds, intertwined in the modern history of the Conservative Party. How they came together would ultimately help to determine the fate of a nation.

May went to a series of local schools, both state and private (the private school, St Juliana's, charged fees of £25 a term, about £500 in today's money). At the one she liked best, Holton Park, a girl's grammar, she became interested in politics. Within a year of her arrival Oxfordshire County Council decreed it should become a comprehensive, and it was merged with the local boys' school. By the time it was turned into Wheatley Park Sixth Form she was confident enough to announce, in front of her classmates and teachers, that she intended to become Britain's first woman prime minister. Cameron, at Eton, made it clear that he wanted to be prime minister one day too. (I can testify to that, as I was there at the same time.) In his case, the ambition seemed presumptuous but plausible. At Wheatley Park, May's ambition struck her contemporaries as nothing more than quaint. When Thatcher beat her to it in 1979, May was working as a junior analyst at the Bank of England and is reported to have been seriously aggrieved. Her attitude, back then, must have seemed absurd. Not now.

In 2011, when she was home secretary, May contributed the foreword to a book by a local historian containing memories of an Oxfordshire grammar school education. Her reminiscences describe a very particular milieu, long gone: 'From sherbet fountains to Corona, from Tommy Steele to *Z Cars*, from stodgy puddings to Vesta curries; and that's not to mention the education.' This is a world of which people like Cameron – and me – would have been wholly ignorant, growing up a decade later with The Smiths and *Smash Hits*, *Not the Nine O'Clock News* and *Space Invaders*, not to mention the cosseting of our very expensive education.

Like Cameron, May went to Oxford, though in her case there was nothing inevitable about it. Unlike the politically ambitious boys who gravitated towards PPE, she chose to read geography. She did seek to make her mark in the Union and gained a reputation as an earnest, competent speaker. But she didn't rise in Union politics and had to make do with the presidency of Oxford's second debating club, the Edmund Burke Society, whose set-piece occasions were meant to be more light-hearted. She presided with a meat tenderiser in place of a gavel; the motions she chose for debate included 'That this House thanks Heaven for little girls'. Her boyfriend, Philip

May, who was two years below her, succeeded her as president of the Edmund Burke and went on, unlike his future wife, to become president of the Union in an election where he saw off more fancied candidates – including Damian Green and Alan Duncan, both future Conservative ministers – who were too busy squabbling to notice the threat he posed. Philip May presided over the Union in the spirit of his girlfriend. For his farewell debate he chose the topic of the professionalisation of sport and invited Theresa back to team up with him against Bobby Charlton and Malcolm Turnbull, another ambitious student, and the future prime minister of Australia.

May's Oxford wasn't Cameron's. She went to church every Sunday. She didn't drink much, and in any case couldn't afford to. Her idea of a good time was to watch *The Goodies*, which as one of her university friends puts it, 'was our sense of humour'. Prince spells it out: 'There were no drugs and none of the alcohol-fuelled debauches enjoyed by the Bullingdon Club boys David Cameron and Boris Johnson.' Cameron took his PPE degree and made a brief career in PR, biding his time until a safe seat became available. May, who had no formal economic training, went to work at the Bank of England before going to the City. She also got stuck into local politics, becoming a Tory councillor in Merton, a large and diverse borough that includes the All-England Tennis Club in Wimbledon as well as some of the most deprived parts of Mitcham. Cameron's path to Parliament was the one that would soon become conventional for his generation: special adviser (to Norman Lamont when he was chancellor), then a bit of media work (for Carlton Television), all eased by the lubricant of personal connections. May took the old-fashioned route. She fought two losing campaigns in safe Labour seats before finally securing the nomination for the winnable constituency of Maidenhead in 1995. Strikingly, in the two campaigns she lost she declined to take part in hustings with her Labour opponents, choosing instead to focus on canvassing the Tory vote. Canvassing – whether in local or national elections – remains her preferred way of doing politics. Given the chance, she likes to knock on doors, even as prime minister.

May won the plum nomination for Maidenhead ahead of three hundred other applicants, among them the twenty-nine-year-old Cameron, chancing his luck. This is one of the few occasions before she succeeded him as prime minister when he would have noticed her without her necessarily noticing him. Cameron didn't even make the shortlist, which included Philip Hammond, May's future chancellor, whom she saw off in the final three. She was forty when she became an MP, at the 1997 election. At the same time Cameron fought, and lost, the seat of Stafford, which the Tories had been hoping to hold before Blair blew all such hopes away. By that point May had been married to Philip for close on twenty years. They had no children, something she has since revealed was not a matter of choice. Both her parents died when she was in her early twenties: her father in a car crash and her mother of multiple sclerosis a few months later. It had been, for want of a better word, a struggle. But she got there.

The four-year head start May had on Cameron turned out to count for very little. Blair's landslide victory had left Tory numbers in the Commons greatly depleted, and talent was thin on the ground. Women were barely represented at all – there were just thirteen female Tory MPs, compared with more than a hundred on the Labour benches. Still, May wasn't favoured by circumstance. Her talents were acknowledged, but they were also pigeonholed: she was seen as a hard worker, a dogged campaigner and a joiner-in. In the face of Blair's massive majority and seemingly unshakeable personal popularity, opposition for the Tories meant the grinding work of holding the government to account line by line in committees. May was recognised to be good at this and good at standing her ground in the chamber. Yet there was a sense that the people who were busy keeping the show on the road weren't the ones who would ultimately revive the party's fortunes. She was marked down as someone suited for middle-ranking jobs that required tenacity rather than flair. William Hague promoted her to shadow secretary of state for education, a high-profile position for a newcomer but also traditionally a department that the Tories felt suited a female touch. The fact that Thatcher had been there before her didn't mean the Tory high command was thinking of May as a future leader. It meant it was thinking of her as another woman.

May got an opportunity to escape this strait-jacket when Iain Duncan Smith made her party chairman in 2002, a decision that was widely seen at the time as smacking of desperation. She took advantage of the profile the role gave her to do two things that have helped shape her image ever since. For her first party conference as chairman she wore a pair of leopard-print kitten heels. And in her speech she told the assembled Tories some essential home truths. 'You know what some people call us? The nasty party.' Only once she became prime minister did both these moves look like essential steps on her path to the top. Back then they served to reinforce rather than to overturn the doubts many Tories had about her. Her choice of footwear confirmed the view of the sceptics that she was, in Tory-speak, 'a colour supplement politician'. Her blunt address, however unarguable the truth it contained, struck her colleagues as simply giving Labour another stick to beat them with. Duncan Smith never really trusted her after that, and when his disastrous tenure as leader was brought to an end a year later, she was moved on by his successor, Michael Howard, who restored her to the ranks of heavy-lifters rather than heavy-hitters by making her shadow secretary of state for transport and the environment. In 2004 two members of the intake of 2001, Cameron and George Osborne, joined her in the shadow cabinet. Both quickly established themselves as part of the leader's inner circle, from which she was excluded. In three years, and seemingly without having to do much more than show up, Cameron had got closer to the summit than May had in seven. She resented it. She may also have resented the fact that Witney, where Cameron had landed on his feet, was looking like a safer bet than Maidenhead, which had become a prime target for the resurgent Lib Dems. May had to take time out to pound the streets of her constituency, this time not only by choice but also by necessity. Meanwhile, Cameron had his feet up on the desk awaiting his moment.

When Howard stepped down as leader following his general election defeat to Blair in 2005, May fully intended to stand to succeed him. She trailed the idea; she sounded out her colleagues; she prepared policy positions that went beyond her familiar briefs. Not only did Cameron beat her to it, but he didn't even notice she was putting herself forward. She might as well have been a ghost. She found that her experience and unquestioned competence counted for little with her fellow MPs. It seems she was only able to secure the backing of a handful of them – it may have been as few as two – and in the end she didn't even announce her candidacy formally. She pulled back before she could step out from behind the curtain. Howard still claims to be unaware that she had wanted to put her hat in the ring. Cameron saw off his main rivals – Kenneth Clarke and David Davis – and then offered May a job, as shadow leader of the House, which confirmed her place somewhere in the middle of the pecking order. She was good at it – it suited her organisational abilities – but she was done little good by it. Meanwhile, almost without noticing where they had come from, Cameron started to adopt positions for which May had diligently prepared the ground. What else was his modernising agenda other than an attempt to lay to rest the 'nasty party' tag? After her aborted leadership bid May started an organisation called Women2Win, designed to redress the massive gender imbalance in the parliamentary party. Cameron folded it into his A-list strategy, which recommended priority candidates for parliamentary seats, thereby reducing it in some people's eyes to a PR exercise. In 2002, when still shadowing education, May had come up with the idea of 'free schools', designed to allow parents and teachers in the state system to escape the shackles of local government control. It had gone nowhere under Duncan Smith. Cameron and his shadow education secretary, Michael Gove, soon claimed the idea as their own.

||||

May got her one big stroke of luck in 2010 with the formation of the coalition government. Had Cameron won an outright majority, she might well have remained stuck where she was. But she was blessed by the fact that the Lib Dems were just as bad as the Tories at promoting women. The negotiating teams for both coalition partners were all-male affairs, and before the ink was dry the boys suddenly noticed that they needed a woman for one of the top jobs. So May was offered the post of home secretary. Normally inscrutable after years of disappointment, she was flabbergasted. Andy Coulson, Cameron's communications chief, reported her face when she was offered the job as 'something to behold'. When he congratulated her, she replied: 'I can't quite believe it.' In post, she soon developed a distinctive governing style. The point of the coalition was meant to be negotiation between the two parties to find positions both could live with. May didn't do negotiation; in the words of Eric Pickles, one of her cabinet colleagues, she is not a 'transactional' politician. She takes a position and then she sticks to it, seeing it as a matter of principle that she delivers on what she has committed to. This doesn't mean that she is a conviction politician. Often she arrives at a position reluctantly after much agonising – as home secretary she became notorious for being painfully slow to decide on matters over which she had personal authority. Many of the positions she adopts are ones she has inherited, seeing no option but to make good on other people's promises. This has frequently brought her into conflict with the politicians from whom she inherited these commitments. By making fixed what her colleagues regarded as lines in the sand, she drove some of them mad.

Her time in the coalition was remarkable for the number of bitter personal disputes she had with fellow ministers. Many of these were over the issue of immigration. She came into a department that was pre-committed by the Conservative manifesto to bringing annual immigration down to 'the tens of thousands' from the hundreds of thousands it had been under Labour. Her colleagues, including Cameron, didn't seem to have thought about whether this was a realistic target and assumed that, if it wasn't, it would have to be fudged. May had no intention of fudging it, to the increasing consternation of the people who had landed her with the task. It is far from clear she believed it was good policy. That wasn't the issue. It was now her policy and she would see it through. In 2011 this brought her into conflict with the justice secretary, Kenneth Clarke, who mocked the conference speech in which she had laid into the Human Rights Act by raising the case of 'the illegal immigrant who cannot be deported because – and I am not making this up – he had a pet cat'. Clarke called her attitude 'child-like and laughable'. She never forgave him. In the same year she had a public falling-out with Vince Cable at the Department for Business, Innovation and Skills, who thought her inflexible approach to limiting the numbers of overseas students was stifling innovation and competitiveness. She got her special advisers to brief against him. Subsequently, he said: 'The Home Office propaganda, which she promoted, fed on itself. It meant she was locked into a very hard line position which she couldn't retreat from even if she wanted to.'

In 2012 Osborne gave her a withering rebuke at cabinet over the case of a Chinese businessman he had been cultivating who had been strip-searched by border officers at Heathrow before getting on a flight back to China. In response May simply sat and stared. 'She couldn't stand him after that,' a cabinet colleague reported later. Her worst feud was with Michael Gove. This was only secondarily about immigration. Their antipathy came to a head in 2014 over the question of radicalisation in schools. Gove, who is much more of an ideas politician, thought May's approach was fixated on security issues and that she wasn't doing enough to tackle the deep-seated social causes of alienation. She felt his attitude was grandstanding: it had, in the words of one of her allies, 'more than a whiff of neocon about it'. The briefing and counter-briefing that ensued cost Gove his job as education secretary and May the services of her most trusted adviser, Fiona Hill. But their dispute also had its origins in an incident a year earlier, when Gove had sounded off at a cabinet away-day about a Home Office policy that he had come to see as hopelessly inadequate, the so-called Gang Task Force. This was something May had adopted at Gove's suggestion. Now here he was telling her it was a waste of time. It had been his idea, until he forgot about it and started pushing for something better. She was lumbered with it and had to put up with being accused of inflexibility and a lack of imagination as a result. It isn't hard to see why she might have felt ill used. What she can't have known then, but might have guessed, was that this wouldn't be the last time.

Once May was installed as prime minister, two things about this period became starkly apparent. First, her approach to Brexit would be a continuation of the same pattern. She inherited Brexit. So she would have to deliver it, unlike the supposed big thinkers who conjured it up in the first place. Unnervingly, it's difficult to avoid the conclusion that prioritising the control of immigration over all other considerations, resulting in the fatally flawed deal she put before parliament in December 2018, was her way of trying to show she could complete the task she had been set back in 2010. As Prince puts it, 'The challenge of controlling immigration [as home secretary] would become her most intractable problem and, by her own standard, the one she failed to overcome. In hindsight, the target she was set was probably always unachievable. Long after others had given up, she continued to strive to meet it. As prime minister, she still does.' 'I don't know whose idea the original promise was,' Michael Howard says of the 'tens of thousands' pledge, 'but I rather doubt it was hers. Obviously we couldn't get down to that level without leaving the EU. She did get the non-EU numbers down, not nearly far enough, but [...] she got them moving in the right direction. But we could never get them down to the tens of thousands while we stayed in the EU.'

There has been much speculation about whether May, who nominally campaigned for Remain, was secretly a Leaver all along, just as there has been subsequent speculation that, despite her desperate push to achieve Brexit, she was secretly a Remainer still. The evidence for her supposed duplicity lies not just in the way she has behaved since the referendum but also in the very muted way she conducted herself during the campaign, to the point where she became known inside Downing Street as 'submarine May'. But there is a more straightforward explanation. In 2013 May was slapped down by Cameron's team for straying outside her remit by delivering a speech entitled 'Vision for Britain', which was seen as a transparent leadership pitch. She responded with a self-denying ordinance pledging she would never again as home secretary stray beyond her brief. She stuck to it during the EU referendum, limiting herself to a few half-hearted remarks about the security implications, where the case for Remain was always going to be a little narrow. If Cameron had wanted more from her, then he should have allowed more from her earlier on. Whether or not May ever believed in Brexit is really a secondary issue. For her politics is all about following through.

The other thing that became immediately apparent once she supplanted Cameron is how little her former colleagues appear to have appreciated this. Within twenty minutes of her arrival in Number Ten, May had summoned Osborne to sack him. Accounts of this meeting differ. Osborne's people say it was cordial. But May's people, who included Fiona Hill, by then safely back in the fold, let it be known that the new prime minister gave him a severe dressing down, telling him he had overpromised and underdelivered on the economy. What is clear is that Osborne had little idea how much she loathed him. He had thought that their previous disputes were just part of the cut and thrust of high politics and easily put behind them. That's precisely what she loathed about him. She hates the idea that politics is just a game, which is what she suspects the Cameroons have always believed. Once he was gone, Osborne reciprocated the loathing from his new perch as editor of the London *Standard*. He was reported as saying that he would only be happy when Mrs May was chopped up in bits in his freezer.

Once installed as prime minister, May dispatched Gove with equal relish, telling him she couldn't stomach his betrayal of Boris Johnson in the Tory leadership contest. Many observers were equally surprised when she brought Johnson back as foreign secretary, given that they too had previous from his time as mayor of London, when they had fallen out over his attempt to usurp her authority by purchasing three water cannons from Germany to help keep public order in the capital. The difference was that Johnson never tried to put her in her place; if anything, it was the other way round, after she blocked the use of the water cannons and then told him off about it in the Commons, where he couldn't answer back. The public tends to see Johnson as the ultimate clown politician, all stunts and no substance. That was not the way May saw it. For her it was Cameron, Osborne and Gove who were fundamentally unserious, because they were the ones who made promises they couldn't keep. Johnson had the advantage of never having his promises believed in the first place.

The startling break May made with the administration of her predecessor created the impression that she was not merely his nemesis but his opposite. Cameron was all posh-boy charm and insouciance, flying by the seat of his pants with the aid of his network of well-connected chums. May is earnest and diligent, apparently less opportunistic and more willing to assess things on their merits. One of her cabinet colleagues put it like this: 'Unless I've misunderstood her, I don't think she's calculating. I don't think she'd do something to be politically popular. I'm not saying she's a saint or an angel, but by and large she would do what she would think was right.' But it's not as simple as that. May is much more Cameron's mirror image than she is his antithesis. Politics is just as personal for her as it is for him. Her version builds personal relationships around the virtues of persistence whereas his built them around the advantages of being in the right place at the right time. He was the essay-crisis prime minister. She is the do-your-homework prime minister. That doesn't make her a politician of substance and him a chancer. Both of them are opportunists; it's just that they view the opportunities differently. If anything, her leadership style is even more personality-driven than his. After all, if politics is a game, there have to be some impersonal rules to play by – that's what every game requires. If it's not a game, maybe there are no rules.

Some of May's behaviour as prime minister has been far more cavalier than her reputation for diligence would suggest. Her first party conference speech after taking over was surprisingly reckless, with its pledge not simply to look after ordinary working people but to take on the 'citizens of nowhere', who 'don't understand what the very word "citizenship" means'. The speech was drafted for her by Nick Timothy, the special adviser on whom she had come to depend, along with Fiona Hill; the two served as her joint chiefs of staff. Timothy, like May, is a devotee of grammar schools because he had a good experience at one himself. So they promoted grammar schools. How is that way of deciding government policy any less a product of personal experience than Cameron's reliance on a coterie of Old Etonians? Cameron has always been pretty good at concealing his contempt for his opponents. May has difficulty containing her vitriol, which sometimes spills out in public. When she collected the *Spectator*'s Politician of the Year award at the end of 2016, at an event hosted by Osborne, she turned up in a hard hat and hi-vis jacket to make fun of his habit of being photographed in the same garb at every opportunity. In her acceptance speech, she referred to a passage in the recently published book by Cameron's communications director, Craig Oliver, in which he described 'retching in the street' after Britain voted to leave the EU. 'Most of us experienced it too,' May said, 'when we saw his name on the resignation honours list.' It's easy to imagine her thinking that and not hard to picture her saying it among friends. But it's quite something that she spelled it out in front of the press.

May's most reckless decision was the one she took in April 2017, when she called a general election in order to strengthen her hand in the Brexit negotiations. It did not look especially reckless at the time, given that she was 20 points ahead in some opinion polls. But as that lead shrank to just 2 per cent on election day, it looked foolhardy to the point of being potentially fatal. The campaign brought out the worst in her as a politician, as she struggled to get beyond her remorselessly repeated talking points ('strong and stable') and to adapt to the growing evidence that this was not a Brexit election after all: given the option of voting to reinforce the result of the referendum the previous year, the voters instead chose to focus on bread-and-butter issues, such as social care, university tuition and housing. May's instinctive preference for avoiding election hustings came back to haunt her when she ducked a televised debate with the other leaders of the main parties, sending her home secretary, Amber Rudd, in her place. The debate turned into a litany of attacks on the government's record. Brexit barely got a look in. May's campaign never really recovered.

Once the result of the election had deprived May's Conservatives of their parliamentary majority, she was able to stay in office only by making the kinds of concessions she hated. First, she had to dispense with the services of Hill and Timothy, who carried the can for the debacle. Second, she had to bring Gove back into the government, in order to bolster her Brexiteer credentials. Third, she had to work remorselessly towards the fixed timetable of Britain's pre-agreed exit from the EU on 29 March 2019, on the grounds that the best justification for her continuing as prime minister was that there was not enough time to make a change. Yet her essential character as a politician was unaltered. Over the following eighteen months more than twenty members of her government resigned, including Boris Johnson, declaring her plans unworkable and her inflexibility infuriating. For such a relatively colourless politician she has managed to provoke enormous animus on her own side. Osborne was not alone in reaching for murderous metaphors to describe his feelings for her. Her fellow Tory MPs have talked of 'measuring her for her coffin' and asked her to 'supply her own noose'. One said, in the autumn of 2018: 'The moment is coming when the knife gets heated, stuck in her front and twisted. She will be dead soon.' But she wasn't, not yet. She kept going, doggedly on. All the while, as she worked to sell her seemingly unsellable Brexit deal, she clung fast to her commitment to ending the free movement of people as the one non-negotiable part of Brexit, leaving almost everything else up for grabs. In other words, she was still determined to make good on the task she set herself back in 2010, to be the politician who showed the posh boys that it was possible to get the job done, so long as you stuck at it.

The more beleaguered and alone May appeared, the greater the grudging admiration felt for her by some sections of the public, who came to view her as a decent woman beset by men. She never traded on her gender – beyond using her taste in fashion to mark herself out from the crowd – but at the same time she has never repudiated it either. Her preference for the company of women is one of the many things that distinguish her from the politician to whom she has been most often compared. Anne Jenkin, who helped set up Women2Win with May, says of the two: 'Thatcher was the outsider. She was a man's woman, and that was the secret of her success. She liked men; she liked men more than she liked women. And I don't think that's the case with Theresa.' May is also, as far as one can tell, strikingly uncorrupt. She emerged not just unscathed but enhanced from the expenses scandal in 2009, when it was revealed that she had claimed well under her allowance and was one of the most frugal members of the Commons. In the words of one of her colleagues, she was 'an expenses saint'. Truly, she has never been in it for herself.

The voters never really warmed to May, but some did learn to respect her. What's more, she gives a strong impression of respecting them, or at least having no desire to judge them by any standards other than their own. It is often said of democratic politics that the question voters ask of any leader is: 'Do I like this person?' But it seems more likely that the question at the back of their minds is: 'Would this person like me?' Cameron did OK on that score – better than Ed Miliband – because many voters suspected he would at least be polite and try to conceal any awkwardness he felt. But May is especially good at appearing non-judgemental by the standards of the political elite. Weirdly, she has this in common with Trump, with whom she perhaps shares more than meets the eye. Trump too, for all his manifold unpleasantness, does a good job of seeming to be open-minded when it comes to his voting public: he might shock some of them, but they don't really shock him. He is unspeakable to his fellow politicians, to the press, to his employees, to immigrants and to the women who are unfortunate enough to appear to him worth coveting. But to anyone who doesn't fall into those categories he might seem like someone it wouldn't be too painful to hang out with.

What May lacked, in the end, were the qualities possessed by her predecessor, the man who landed her with this enormous mess in the first place. Getting through Brexit successfully was always likely to require a certain amount of insouciance, which the essay crisis prime minister had in spades. The risk with May was that she would end up drowning in the homework. As so often in politics, the roles seem to have been handed out the wrong way round. May might have been a far better person than Cameron or Osborne to lead the Remain campaign, and had she done so, Britain might still be in the EU: she could have shown the public she took seriously their concerns over immigration. But either Cameron or Osborne might have done a far better job at negotiating Britain's departure. What is the Brexit negotiation if not a game? Johnson showed how it could be played. So long as May remained determined to treat it as a war of attrition, with no goal in the end except to see it through, it was always likely to end badly for her and for all those who refused to break with her approach.

11

DONALD TRUMP

SOME POLITICAL THEORISTS dislike the term 'office politics', on the grounds that the familiarity of the first word diminishes the significance of the second. Sure, they say, all workplaces contain their share of plots and vendettas, backstabbers and arse-lickers, people on the way up and all the ones they've trampled to get there. But actual politics is about more than that: the power it brings extends well beyond the immediate working environment. The early twentieth-century German legal theorist Carl Schmitt, who wanted to prevent the concept of the 'political' from becoming shorthand for any and all human conflict, no matter how petty, argued that the true mark of a political contest is that the stakes are existential.

This was not Existentialism – Schmitt wasn't in the business of trying to help individuals find their own meaning in a meaningless world. What he meant was that in a truly political struggle the way of life of an entire community has to be on the line. The job of the political leader is to decide on what Schmitt called 'the friend/enemy distinction': who we can live with, and who we can't. He meant it literally: if we can't live with them, we might have to kill them. Schmitt was, for a time, a Nazi, which means that his view is, if anything, even grimmer than it sounds. But it does make clear that squabbling over who gets to sit on the next appointments committee doesn't necessarily deserve to be called politics. So how come office battles often feel all-consuming? It's like the old joke about academic life: 'Why are the disputes so poison-ous? Because the stakes are so low.'

One of the remarkable features of the Trump presidency is the way he turns these arguments on their head. No one could doubt that having Trump in the White House is an exis-tential matter: the president's decisions have the potential to bring many ways of life to an end, including our own. The stakes could hardly be higher. Why, then, does reading about it so often feel like reading about any other dysfunctional work-place? The relentless backstabbing and arse-licking seem out of kilter with the seriousness of the situation. It makes for a deeply strange and curiously familiar environment. It is almost impossible to imagine what it would be like to work in the West Wing under Trump, given how far removed it currently is from anything that went on there before. Yet anyone who has ever worked with a narcissistic boss drunk on his or her own power will recognise it at once. The pettiness of Trump-world is like the pettiness of our own world, but with nuclear weapons.

Take this description of the office away-day from hell, sup-plied by Bob Woodward in his book *Fear*, which tells the gossipy inside story of Trump's first year in office. Tired of their boss's inability to understand that his impetuous decisions might have destructive ramifications for the international order, the secretary of defense, Jim Mattis, and chief economic adviser, Gary Cohn, decided that what was needed was a change of scene. So in July 2017 they brought Trump to the Pentagon and arranged for a policy session to take place in its secure meeting room, known as 'the Tank'. 'The Tank had its appeal,' Woodward writes. 'Trump loved the room. Sometimes known as the Gold Room for its carpets and curtains, it is ornate and solemn, essentially a private, high-security retreat reflecting decades of history.' So far, so good. Knowing that the president is a reluctant reader with a very limited attention span, Mattis and Cohn arranged a series of presentations to keep things visual and simple: maps of American commitments around the world, charts of import and export data, pictures of warships. Cohn's obsession was to get Trump to understand that trade deficits don't have to mean the US is losing: he wanted the president to know that it's possible to be in deficit and still to be growing the economy. But Trump soon loses patience. 'I don't want to hear that, it's bullshit.'

Steve Bannon, at this point the president's chief strategist, and therefore someone who had to be invited along, decided to jump in. What's the value in defending the international order if America's allies won't give anything back? Trump had made it clear he wanted to tear up the Iran nuclear deal.

> 'Is one of your fucking great allies up in the European Union going to back the president?' Bannon wants to know. 'Give me one guy. One country. One company. Who's going to back sanctions?' Now Trump perked up. 'That's what I'm talking about,' Trump said. 'He just made my point. You talk about all these guys as allies. There's not an ally up there. Answer Steve's question. Who's going to back us?'

No one could answer Bannon's question, so the president moved on to Afghanistan, where he couldn't understand why he was spending so much money for so little return. 'When are we going to start winning some wars? We've got these charts. When are we going to win some wars? Why are you jamming this down my throat?' The charts weren't helping. In fact they were making things worse. 'You should be killing guys,' Trump told the trained killers in the room. 'You don't need a strategy to kill people.'

By this point it was clear that the meeting had backfired horribly. But no one knew how to get out of it. (H. R.

McMaster, Trump's national security adviser, had already guessed which way it was heading and pleaded a family engagement to escape – every away-day has one of those too.) The conversation circled back to trade deals. '"We're upside down" on trade deals, Trump said. "We're underwater on every one of these." The other countries are making money. "Just look at all this stuff up there. We're paying for it all."' Cohn tried to remind him that it was actually good for the US economy. '"I don't want to hear that," Trump replied. "It's all bullshit."' Trump wanted to bring the money home, especially from South Korea. In desperation, Cohn asked him emolliently: 'So, Mr President, what would you need in the region to sleep well at night?' 'I wouldn't need a fucking thing. And I'd sleep like a baby.'

Just reading about this meeting feels intensely claustrophobic. Trump's then chief of staff, Reince Priebus, sums up how unpleasant it was to be present: 'The distrust in the room had been thick and corrosive. The atmosphere was primitive; everyone was ostensibly on the same side, but they had seemed suited up in battle armour, particularly the president. This was what craziness was like.' It is also what a toxic working environment is like. All that's missing is the attempt afterwards to brush it under the carpet and pretend that everyone can carry on as before. And inevitably Trump supplied it. 'The meeting was great,' he told reporters afterwards. 'A very good meeting.'

||||

Under these circumstances, how far should the president's men go in doing his bidding, and how far should they be willing to resist? It is one of the oldest political questions of all – when does disobedience shift from being a crime to being a duty? – and Woodward supplies a showpiece example of how that age-old dilemma can play out under this presidency. Cohn, along with Trump's staff secretary, Rob Porter, conspires to remove a letter from the president's desk to prevent him from signing it. The letter in question was addressed to the president of South Korea, notifying him of Trump's intention to terminate the US–Korea free trade agreement, known as KORUS. For Cohn this would have been a disaster, fatally undermining American security interests in the region. It was also economically illiterate: Trump's attempt to save money would end up costing his country dear. Cohn believed he was acting in the national interest. 'I stole it off his desk [...] I wouldn't let him see it. He's never going to see that document. Got to protect the country.' It makes sense. But it is also absurd. He was acting as though literally taking the issue outside the room is all that's needed to make it go away. The American state is still a vast bureaucratic machine, and all pieces of paper must leave a trail. If this really is all it takes to make the problem disappear, then the US government is no longer a functioning political entity. This is a workplace gone mad.

Woodward's verbatim accounts of meetings and shouting matches – and there aren't many meetings that stop short of becoming a shouting match – are all sourced anonymously, but it's never very difficult to work out who the source is. Anyone who works with people they don't trust and can't stand has a version in their head of how a meeting should have gone and what it would have been good to say. *Esprit d'escalier* is the lingua franca of the Trump White House. For each set-piece occasion Woodward describes there is usually a piece of dialogue that sounds like something someone wishes they had said. No doubt Woodward is faithfully recording what he was told. But what he was told is being remembered by people who have an incentive to appear to have seen through the president's folly and told him so at the time. Often the person in question is Cohn, who is presented as the unspoken hero of this tale. This first draft of history is often self-justification from the people who were there and ended up wishing they'd been somewhere else.

In one meeting, Woodward reports, Cohn lost his patience with Trump and his favoured economic guru, Peter Navarro, who had been reinforcing the president's view that trade deficits mean the US is getting screwed. '"If you just shut the fuck up and listen," Cohn said to both Trump and Navarro, "you might learn something."' The only possible source for this exchange is Cohn. So did he actually say it? Sure he did, in his own mind. Another time Trump claimed to Cohn that the historically low unemployment figures were down to his tariffs policy. '"You're a fucking asshole," Cohn said, half-joking and smacking Trump gently on his arm. Cohn turned to a secret service agent. "I just hit the president. If you want to shoot me, go ahead."' It's the 'half-joking' that's the giveaway: it's precisely what Cohn would tell himself after the event. But it's not just Cohn. At other points the source is clearly Bannon, because he's the one who sounds as though he is telling truth to deranged power. When he catches Trump at one of his golf resorts obsessively watching the talking heads on CNN and brooding over their inability to appreciate his brilliance, Bannon tells him to get out more.

> 'What are you doing? Why do you do this? Cut this off. It's not meaningful. Just enjoy yourself.'
>
> Trump's response would often go like this: 'You see that? That's a fucking lie. Who the fuck's ...'
>
> Bannon would say, 'Go play some slap and tickle with Melania.'

Or at least Bannon would think that. Seriously, who in their right mind would actually say it?

Almost no one in this account comes across as authentically themselves, because each source is replaying the events so as to come out of them with a minimum of dignity. Since there is no dignity to be had in Trump's White House, this often sounds forced and fake. The one person who appears to be himself throughout is the one person whom Woodward acknowledges at the outset did not grant an interview for the book: Trump. The president emerges as a bizarre and brutish character, but his behaviour has a strong streak of consistency. He cannot bear to be wrong and he will never admit defeat. He changes his mind but only because he forgets what he has done. When his opinions are ingrained, they are immovable. In another self-serving anecdote for which Cohn must be the source, Woodward reports this circular exchange:

> Several times Cohn asked the president, 'Why do you have these views?'
>
> 'I just do,' Trump replied. 'I've had these views for 30 years.'
>
> 'That doesn't mean they're right,' Cohn said. 'I had the view for 15 years I could play professional football. Doesn't mean I was right.'

Did Cohn really deliver the punchline to the president's face? Maybe. But Trump definitely delivered the set-up.

None of this means that Trump is impervious to regret. Far from it. The president has a gnawing obsession with having appointed the wrong people to serve him, or having kept others in post too long. It is remarkable how much of his conversation is taken up with hiring and firing. Being Trump, he never believes his judgement was at fault. What he thinks is that he was misled at the job interview stage. Hence the violent, implacable loathing he develops for his attorney general, Jeff Sessions, someone he had gone out of his way to praise ('a great man') in his acceptance speech on election night. The problem comes when Sessions recuses himself from the Russia investigation, paving the way for his deputy, Rod Rosenstein, to appoint Robert Mueller as special counsel. Trump considers it a betrayal, not just because it threatens to undermine his presidency but also because it didn't come up when he offered

Sessions his job. 'How do you take a job and then recuse yourself?' Trump wanted to know. 'If he would have recused himself before the job, I would have said, "Thanks, Jeff, but I'm not going to take you." It's extremely unfair – and that's a mild word – to the president.' As soon as he felt safe to do so, following the 2018 midterms, Trump fired him.

The grievance naturally extends to Mueller, not just because he took the job Rosenstein offered and made Trump's life hell, but because he did it after Trump had decided not to employ him. '"Why was Mueller picked?" Trump asked. "He was just in here and I didn't hire him for the FBI," Trump raged. "Of course he's got an axe to grind with me."' And before Mueller there was James Comey, whom Trump fired as director of the FBI, thereby provoking an enormous and entirely predictable backlash. But Trump can't understand it. He fired him! 'I am the president. I can fire anybody that I want. They can't be investigating me for firing Comey. And Comey deserved to be fired! Everybody hated him. He was awful.' And on and on.

Once Trump decides he doesn't want you, that's meant to be it. You don't come back in through another door. Or at least not unless Trump is the one who opens it. Often he plumps for or against people on a whim, heavily influenced by whether he likes the way they look. Hope Hicks, his impossibly glamorous press secretary, commanded his respect because she cut the kind of figure he expected of his employees. 'She had the two qualities important to Trump,' Woodward writes. 'Loyalty and good looks.' With men, Trump likes a certain physical gravitas, of the kind he believes that he himself has in spades. Rex Tillerson, big and ponderous, got the nod as secretary of state because he had the necessary heft. 'Trump told aides that Tillerson looked the part he would play on the world stage. "A very Trumpian-inspired pick," Kellyanne Conway said on television, promising "big impact".' Meanwhile, John Bolton didn't make the grade after his interview for the role of national security adviser, despite giving just the kind of responses that Trump preferred to hear. 'His answers were fine, but Trump did not like his big, bushy moustache. He didn't look the part.' That said, Tillerson eventually got fired as secretary of state, after it was widely reported that he had called Trump a moron. And in 2018 Bolton became national security adviser, after Trump had fired the hefty, shaven-headed general H. R. McMaster from the post. Bolton still has the moustache.

Even in Schmitt's terms, hiring and firing are part of the essence of politics. When you're in the business of making the friend/enemy distinction, it really does matter who is on the appointments committee. Yet in Trump's case it's more than that: he doesn't have any other register. Granting employment and terminating it are his modus operandi. When he reaches a tricky impasse in a conversation, his way out is to make a job offer. Lindsay Graham, the Republican senator, came to see him to explain that the Afghan war was unwinnable. '"We're going to fail on the political," [Graham] said. A peace settlement with the Taliban was the only way out [...] Trump had a solution. Did Graham want to be the ambassador to Pakistan? "No I don't want to be ambassador to Pakistan," Graham said. They left it at that.' Meanwhile, the extraordinary turnover of senior officials under his presidency, which has already consigned many of the leading characters in this administration to history, is testament to Trump's terminal inability to find any meaningful space between disagreement and dismissal.

Apart from his immediate family, almost the only person who was there at the beginning of the story and has remained by his side throughout is Conway. For anyone wanting to learn how it's done, her job interview to serve as his campaign manager, which took place during the early stages of his bid for the presidency, is a model of how Trump likes to see these things go. He took a shine to her after she came to organise the recording of some campaign ads. He asked her whether she agreed that he was a much better candidate than Hillary Clinton. 'Well, yes, sir,' she replied, 'no poll necessary.'

'Do you think you can run this thing?' he asked.

'What is "this thing"?' she asked. 'I'm running this photo shoot.'

'The campaign,' Trump said. 'The whole thing. Are you willing to not see your kids for a few months?'

She accepted on the spot. 'Sir, I can do that for you. You can win this race. I do not consider myself your peer. I will never address you by your first name.'

Since Conway and Trump were the only two people present for this conversation, Conway must be the source. No wonder Trump likes her so much. Of all the characters in Woodward's book, she is the only one who doesn't seem to set much store by her own dignity.

Later on, scarred by what he saw as the repeated failure of candidates for one job or another to be fully on board with him, he decided to dispense with interviews altogether. Indeed, he even dispensed with the formal job offer and started recruiting by diktat. When Priebus went, driven to the point of no return by Trump's lunatic decision to hire and then fire Anthony Scaramucci as his press secretary over a ten-day period, one of his final acts was to recommend General John Kelly as a possible replacement. Trump said they should mull it over. Then, a few hours later, Priebus got an alert for the latest tweet from @ realdonaldtrump: 'I am pleased to inform you that I have just named General/Secretary John F. Kelly as White House Chief of Staff. He is a Great American.' Priebus got in touch with Kelly, who told him that he first heard about it the same way Priebus did. Kelly had just had to call his wife and 'explain that he had no choice but to accept after being offered one of the most important jobs in the world via tweet'. It was, by Trump's standards, a pretty seamless manoeuvre: no one knew what was happening, so no one had a chance to stitch him up. LBJ might have been proud. Kelly too has now been fired. Still, he lasted longer than most.

||||
||||

Woodward tells his story straight and leaves the reader to draw the moral, though he also makes sure that the moral is not hard to miss. Occasionally he provides some commentary to spell it out. The key passage in the book is this one, which he appends to the story of Priebus's departure and Kelly's arrival:

> The most important part of Trump's world was the ring right outside of the bull's-eye: the people that Trump thought perhaps he should have hired, or who had worked for him and he'd gotten rid of and now thought, maybe I shouldn't have. It was the people who were either there or should have been there, or associates or acquaintances that owed nothing to him and were around him but didn't come in for anything. It was that outside circle that had the most power, not the people on the inside. It wasn't Kelly or Priebus or Bannon.

Trump is haunted by the lingering presence of the hires he should have fired and the fires he should have hired. He spends much of his time railing at these ghosts. Woodward calls it power, but it's more like the opposite of power: these shadowy figures are what stand in the way of anyone else getting anything done.

The people who believe they are part of Trump's inner circle often misunderstand where they fit in, because they mistake proximity for power, even if no one in Trump's world could mistake it for job security. Bannon, for instance, had delusions of grandeur. He is convinced that he was the one who stage-managed Trump's election victory. 'I realised,' he said later, 'I'm the director and he's the actor.' This couldn't be further from the truth. No one can direct Trump because he is incapable of sustaining an act. At another point Bannon decides that he is the impresario and Trump, who can fill any stadium simply by showing up and ad-libbing for a couple of hours, is 'the rock star'. But Trump is no rock star either. He lacks the requisite exuberance. In the end it is impossible to avoid the conclusion that the most familiar impression of Trump is the correct one. The template for this presidency is reality television. The lead character is playing a part that depends on his own words and actions and yet is entirely contrived. The drama is organised around a series of showdowns and confrontations when everything seems to be on the line and yet nothing is really at stake. Each episode ends with some people staying and others being sent home. This seems to matter enormously at the time, and yet it is hard to remember from one week to the next why anyone cared. From one season to the next it is hard even to remember who the main players were, and sometimes the winners are the hardest of all to remember. Yet everyone knows whose show it is. And we can't stop watching.

This could be *The Apprentice*. Even so, something is missing. Struggling through Woodward's account, I had a strong sense that Trump reminded me of someone I had seen regularly on TV, but it wasn't TV's Donald Trump. Then I got it. The working environment this White House brings to mind is a reality show that displays a deeper level of truth by being entirely fictitious. Woodward's book reads more than anything like a mockumentary, and the person Trump most resembles is David Brent from *The Office*. He has the grating inadequacy, the knee-jerk nastiness, the comical self-delusion. But he also has something of the pathos. He even has moments when his inability to see anything beyond the situation at hand is just what the situation needs. Woodward describes the way Trump would speak on the phone to the parents of soldiers killed in action.

'I'm looking at his picture – such a beautiful boy,' Trump said in one call to family members. Where did he grow up? Where did he go to school? Why did he join the service?

'I've got the record here,' Trump said. 'There are reports here that say how much he was loved. He was a great leader.'

Some in the Oval Office had copies of the service records. None of what Trump cited was there. He was just making it up. He knew what the families wanted to hear.

It goes without saying that Trump is a liar. But the lying is not the essence of who he is. It is a product of his neediness, combined with his inability ever to let someone else have the last word. His advisers cannot get him to apologise for anything, because he cannot ever be seen to back down. After the 'grab-them-by-the-pussy' tape was released in the last weeks of the 2016 campaign, Trump refused to admit fault, despite the frantic efforts of Conway and others to get him to read out a statement that said: 'My language was inappropriate, not acceptable for a president.' He throws it out. 'This is bullshit. This is weak. You guys are weak.' They try to reword it. Trump got through two lines and baulked. 'I'm not doing this,' he said. And he didn't. Rudy Giuliani had been among those who tried to get Trump to read a statement of contrition, and when he refused, Giuliani was the only member of his team willing to go on television to defend him. When Jake Tapper of CNN said Trump's words had offered a picture of sexual assault that was 'really offensive on a basic human level', Giuliani could only say: 'Yes, it is.' Afterwards, Trump told his loyal ally: 'Rudy, you're a baby! I've never seen a worse defence of me in my life. They took your diaper off right there. You're like a little baby that needed to be changed. When are you going to be a man?'

On the very rare occasions Trump does offer an apology, it makes things worse. After the white supremacist rally in Charlottesville which left one protester dead and many injured,

Trump initially blamed the violence on both sides. Then, following an outcry, he was persuaded to deliver a statement in which he condemned the neo-Nazis who were responsible. Then following widespread praise for having changed course, he went back to his original position, insisting that 'there are two sides to every story'. He told Porter, who had constructed the act of contrition for him: 'You never make those concessions. You never apologise. I didn't do anything wrong in the first place. Why look weak?' This is the reason Trump's lawyer John Dowd knew Trump must never be allowed to testify before the Mueller inquiry. You cannot put this man on the stand, Dowd says at the end of *Fear*, because Trump is 'a fucking liar'. But liars take the stand all the time. It's because Trump literally does not know when to shut up that he would destroy himself. Dowd eventually quit after Trump insisted he would make an excellent witness. Dowd reminded Trump of the time he gave a deposition to a lawyer in Florida. 'When the lawyer had asked him what he did for a living, it had taken Trump about 16 pages to answer the question.' Those weren't 16 pages of lies. He was shadow-boxing the ghosts in his head, with no one to stop him.

BOOKS DISCUSSED

LYNDON JOHNSON

Robert A. Caro, *The Years of Lyndon Johnson: The Passage of Power* (Knopf, 2012)

MARGARET THATCHER

Charles Moore, *Margaret Thatcher: The Authorised Biography*, vol. 1, *Not for Turning* (Allen Lane, 2013)

BILL CLINTON

Taylor Branch, *The Clinton Tapes: Wrestling History in the White House* (Simon & Schuster, 2009)

George Stephanopoulos, *All Too Human: A Political Education* (Little, Brown & Co., 1999)

TONY BLAIR

Tony Blair, *A Journey* (Hutchinson, 2010)

Peter Mandelson, *The Third Man: Life at the Heart of New Labour* (Harper Press, 2010)

GORDON BROWN

Gordon Brown, *My Life, Our Times* (Bodley Head, 2017)

Alistair Darling, *Back from the Brink: 1000 Days at No. 11* (Atlantic Books, 2011)

THE ONES WHO GOT AWAY

Andrew Young, *The Politician: An Insider's Account of John Edwards's Pursuit of the Presidency and the Scandal that Brought Him Down* (St. Martin's Press, 2010)

John Heilemann and Mark Halperin, *Game Change: Obama and the Clintons, McCain and Palin, and the Race of a Lifetime* (Harper Collins, 2010)

BARACK OBAMA

Ben Rhodes, *The World As It Is: Inside the Obama White House* (Bodley Head, 2018)

BLAIR REDUX

Tom Bower, *Broken Vows: Tony Blair – The Tragedy of Power* (Faber, 2016)

DAVID CAMERON

David Cameron, *For the Record* (William Collins, 2019)

THERESA MAY

Rosa Prince, *Theresa May: The Enigmatic Prime Minister* (Biteback, 2017)

DONALD TRUMP

Bob Woodward, *Fear: Trump in the White House* (Simon & Schuster, 2018)

AFTERWORD

ALL THE ESSAYS IN THIS BOOK, with the exception of the introduction, were originally published in the *London Review of Books* over the course of the last ten years. They are ordered here in rough sequence of the events and periods they describe, rather than the order in which they first appeared. Each essay has been substantially revised and updated. This paperback edition includes one new essay, about David Cameron, based on his memoirs, which appeared after a long delay in September 2019. When I was making the revisions to the other essays, before the original publication of this book, the ultimate fate of the leaders whose story I tell in the final two chapters was not yet resolved. Donald Trump's political future still remains wide open as I write now. But Theresa May's fate is long since sealed.

May's career ended in ultimate failure, broken by Brexit. She was unable to find an agreement that could satisfy either the doubters in her own party, of whom there were many, or the potential converts to her cause among the Labour opposition, of whom there turned out to be very few. Her determination to press on with her chosen course of action in the face of vanishing support came to seem delusional. By the time she quit, it appeared that she might take the Conservative Party down with her. The party had received just 8.8 per cent of the national vote in the European Parliament elections that were held in May 2019 as a direct result of her failure to get her Brexit deal through. It was far from clear that any alternative leader could revive its fortunes. Yet just six months later, May's successor Boris Johnson won a general election – one that he had engineered – with a majority of 80 in the House of Commons and with 43.6 per cent of the national vote, the largest majority and the highest Conservative vote share since the heyday of Margaret Thatcher.

Johnson had achieved what May couldn't. He found a new Brexit deal where she had insisted that was impossible; he united his party when she had suggested that it was riven by disloyalty; he routed Jeremy Corbyn after she had, in a final act of desperation, sought to make a deal with him. Johnson's remarkable triumph shows, among other things, how much a prime minister's ultimate reputation depends on who or what comes next. Thanks to Johnson, May will not go down in history as the woman who broke the Conservative Party. But she will be remembered as the leader who failed to do what her successor, a man she so often derided, soon managed. Johnson has saved May from ignominy. But he has almost certainly guaranteed her the condescension of future historians.

When she finally stepped down, May ended her resignation speech outside 10 Downing Street with a characteristic note of quiet defiance. 'I will shortly leave the office that it has been the honour of my life to hold – the second female Prime minister but certainly not the last. I do so with no ill-will but with enormous and enduring gratitude to have had the opportunity to serve the country I love.' Then she wept.

Some commentators suggested at the time that if she had shown more of that raw emotion earlier, her fate might have been different. But it is hard to see how: no amount of tears would have altered the toxic brew that Brexit had become under her premiership. Other commentators complained that she left Downing Street as much of a mystery as she had entered it.

Nearly three years at the top had failed to show us who she really was or what she truly believed. My argument has been that this gets things the wrong way round. High office was never going to reveal the person we had not seen before. She left the top job the same as she had arrived: a dutiful, relentless, unimaginative, inflexible, hard to budge politician. Her fall was in keeping with her rise. She stuck it out until there was nowhere else to go. Even her final remarks harked back to her political beginnings. The Cotswold girl who had believed she could be the first female prime minister was there to remind us that at least she had been the second. No one could take that away from her.

What May's premiership revealed were the limits of the office she held. A personality like hers could not find the authority needed to bend others to her will. Once she had lost her majority in parliament – but likely even before that – she discovered that dogged determination was not enough. Brexit required more chutzpah and more flair, qualities that Johnson was able to provide. May had wanted to emulate Thatcher, whose own personality had suited the office she held and the times in which she found herself. But May's personality did not suit her circumstances. She was ultimately out of time, in all senses.

Johnson too would like to emulate Thatcher, and with his election victory he has come closer than May ever did. But in Johnson's case it is more complicated than that. He also appears to be emulating Trump. In June 2018, after he quit as May's foreign secretary, he said: 'Imagine Trump doing Brexit … He'd go in bloody hard … There'd be all sorts of breakdowns, all sorts of chaos. Everyone would think he'd gone mad. But, actually, you might get somewhere. It's a very, very good thought.' This thought, in the context of British politics, is something new. As a result, British politics may now be approaching a fork in the road: Thatcher or Trump? In other words, do you test the limits of the office of prime minister or do you choose to ignore them altogether?

During his early tenure as prime minister Johnson has done a bit of both, suggesting that perhaps it does not have to be a choice. During the first few months of his premiership he found himself stymied in Parliament and blocked by the courts. His prorogation of Parliament was declared unlawful by the Supreme Court and his early attempts to force a general election were repeatedly rebuffed. For a while it appeared he had nowhere to go. Yet in the end, the opposition parties in Parliament bent to his will and allowed him the election that provided him with a way out from his predicament. It meant that any choice between testing the rules and ignoring them was forestalled. What would have happened if Johnson had not been able to force an election and instead had faced and lost a vote of no confidence in the Commons? Under those circumstances, it was suggested in anonymous briefings to the press, he might still refuse to quit. He would dare the Queen to force him out. At that point, the question would have found its answer: not Thatcher, but Trump. But the question was never finally put. So we do not know.

Johnson has also shown that he is not yet willing to buck another trend described in this book, which is to see Lyndon Johnson – and specifically Robert Caro's LBJ – as a template of political leadership. When running to succeed May as Conservative party leader, Johnson chose as his campaign manager Grant Shapps, who let it be known that he kept a copy of Caro's life of LBJ by his bed, and used it as his campaign bible. The ruthless and efficient way the seemingly bumbling Boris managed to dispatch his rivals – and even to redistribute the votes of his parliamentary colleagues between them so as to ensure he faced his preferred opponent Jeremy Hunt in the run-off rather than the more dangerous Michael Gove – was distinctly Johnsonian (in the LBJ sense). So it is possible that the question I ask at the end of the introduction – are we seeing the close of the period of political leadership dominated by the model of Caro's LBJ? – has also found an answer of sorts in the other Johnson: not yet.

But that, of course, would be to ignore Trump himself, who is not interested in Caro's life of Johnson, or indeed in the lives of any of his predecessors, barring perhaps Lincoln, who appears to be the only one whom he considers fit to compare himself with. Trump remains a politician apart, quite unlike the others I discuss in this book. As I write now, at the start of Trump's impeachment trial in the US Senate and a week before the first presidential primary, the question of who will be chosen to face him in the 2020 general election looms large over US politics and over the fate of the world. The Democrats are facing some familiar questions of democratic political judgment: do they choose the best campaigner or the best candidate? Do they prioritise the candidate or the programme? Do they try to second-guess the wider electorate or do they go with their own tribal instincts? I have no idea how this will play out. But at the end of the current electoral cycle it is at least possible that the question that was never asked of Boris Johnson will be asked in another form of Trump instead. If the election is close, and if Trump loses narrowly, say by a few thousand votes in a crucial swing state, or by a handful of delegates in the electoral college, will he step down, as the rules of the game say he must? Or will he resist and refuse to accept the result? Might some proxies in the electoral college follow his lead? And if so, what happens then? Again, we cannot know. But we will be able to say with more certainty that American democracy has entered a new phase in its relationship with political leadership. Not leaderless democracy. But something like its opposite.

I am very grateful to the editors at the *London Review of Books* for their contribution to these essays, both by asking me to write them in the first place and for their subsequent editorial guidance. I am also very grateful to Andrew Franklin and Penny Daniel at Profile, and to my agent Peter Straus, for enabling them to appear in book form.

January 2020